The Narragansett Blue Book

~ Fully ~ Illustrated ~

1896

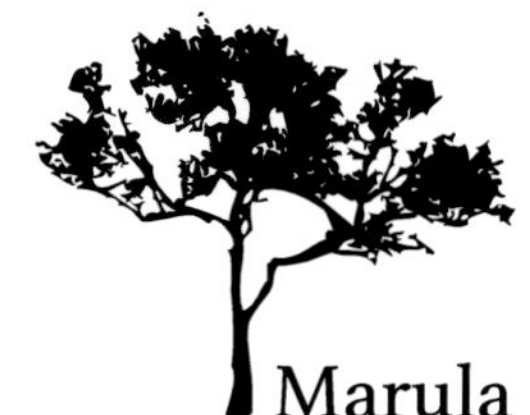

An imprint of Arcadia Publishing

The Narragansett Blue Book
A Summer Souvenir and Guide for the Principal Resorts and Cities on and about Narragansett Bay
by James Allan Reid

A Marula Historical Reprint
Originally published in 1896

Published by Arcadia Publishing
Charleston SC

ISBN 978-0-7385-9469-9

Printed in the United States of America

For all general information contact Arcadia Publishing at:
Telephone 843-853-2070
Fax 843-853-0044
E-mail sales@arcadiapublishing.com
For customer service and orders:
Toll-Free 1-888-313-2665

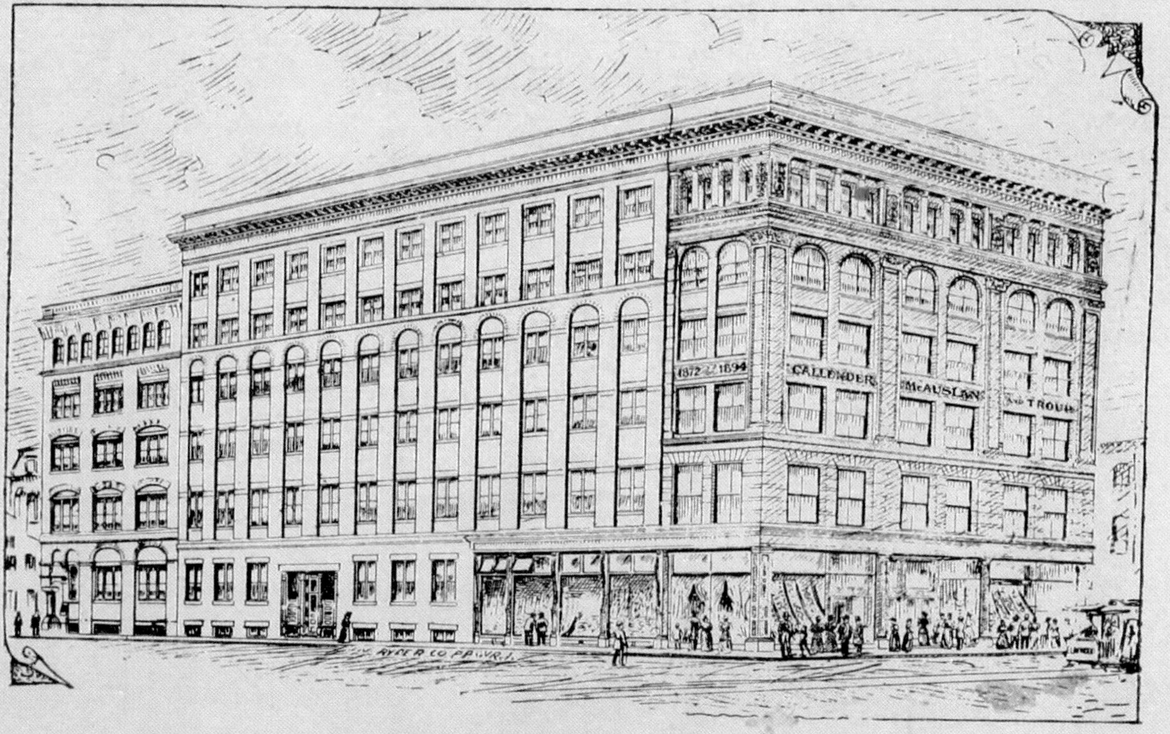

THE BOSTON STORE

Callender, McAuslan & Troup Company, Providence

Some Typewriters write in Sight.
Some print direct. The

Williams

What other Typewriters would be,
The Williams IS.

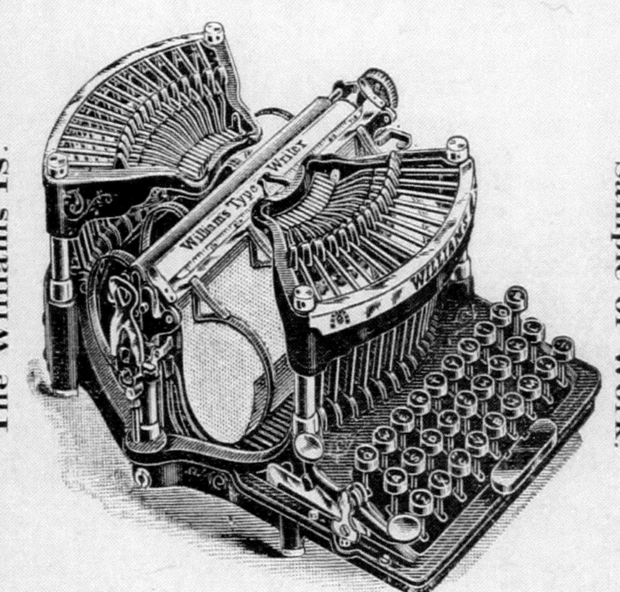

Get Descriptive Pamphlet and
Sample of Work.

Is the only machine in the World
to do both

GOLD MEDAL AND HIGHEST AWARD.
Atlanta. San Francisco. Amsterdam.

THE AMERICAN BOOK EXCHANGE, R. I. Agents,
146 Westminster Street, Providence, R. I.

THE NARRAGANSETT BLUE BOOK

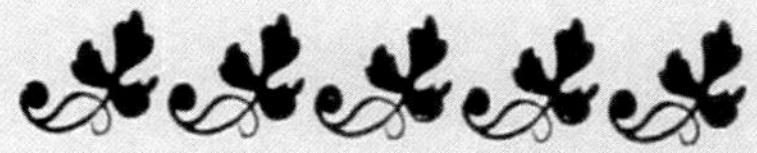

A SUMMER SOUVENIR AND GUIDE FOR THE PRINCIPAL RESORTS AND CITIES ON AND ABOUT

Narragansett Bay

THE HOTELS RESTAURANTS RAILROADS STEAMBOATS AND THE BEST BUSINESS HOUSES

Fully Illustrated

Providence, R. I.:
Published by THE AMERICAN BOOK EXCHANGE
Francis Building 146 Westminster Street
1896

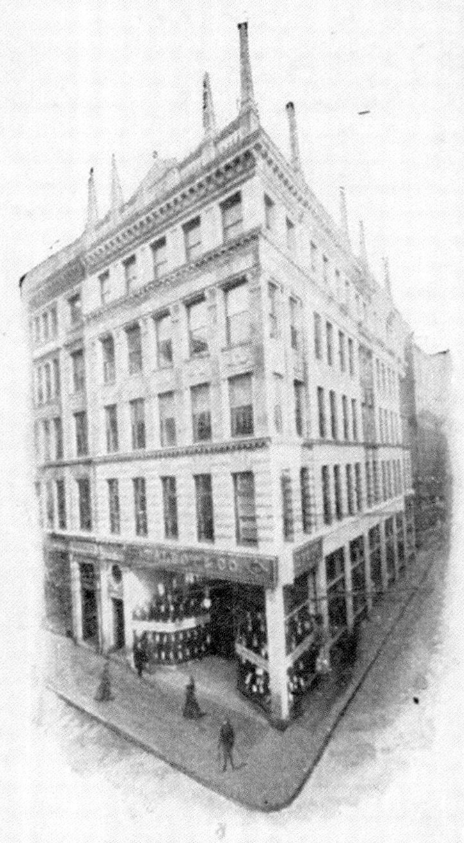

The Francis Building
Home of the American Book Exchange
146 Westminster Street

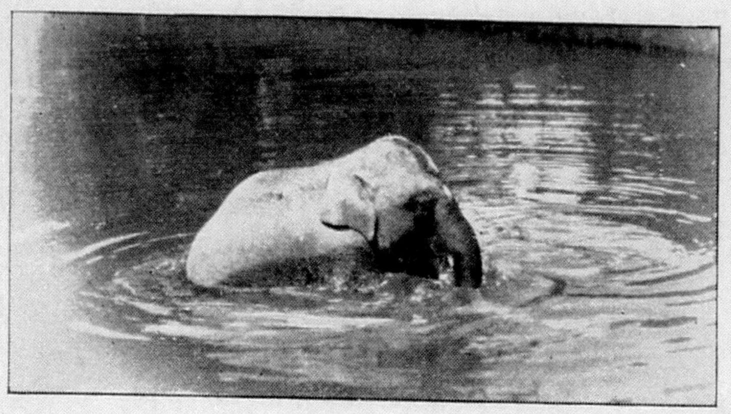

THE BABY ROGER'S FIRST SWIM.

☘INTRODUCTION☘

☘☘☘

☘☘☘☘ The New England coast is penetrated by many charming bays whose shores are lined with popular resorts for the delectation and refreshment of summer sojourners. The chief of all, and the most attractive, is our own Narragansett Bay. ☘ It is favored with a great variety of scenery. ::: On its headwaters and tributaries are three of the brightest cities in New England; at the end of its largest island is located Newport, the most noted of America's watering places, and with Narragansett Pier on the main, Block Island thirty miles out to sea, and the numerous smaller but famous outing-spots in and about its shores a day's excursion or a summer's rest may be enjoyed with delight by rich or poor. The facilities for transportation by boat, rail or electrics are adequate.☘☘☘☘☘☘☘For the river excursionist and for those taking their breath of fresh air by means of the electrics ☘THE BLUE BOOK☘ will point out the most pleasing trips, the cost will be counted, and the numerous features for the eye to feast upon will be pictured in its pages.

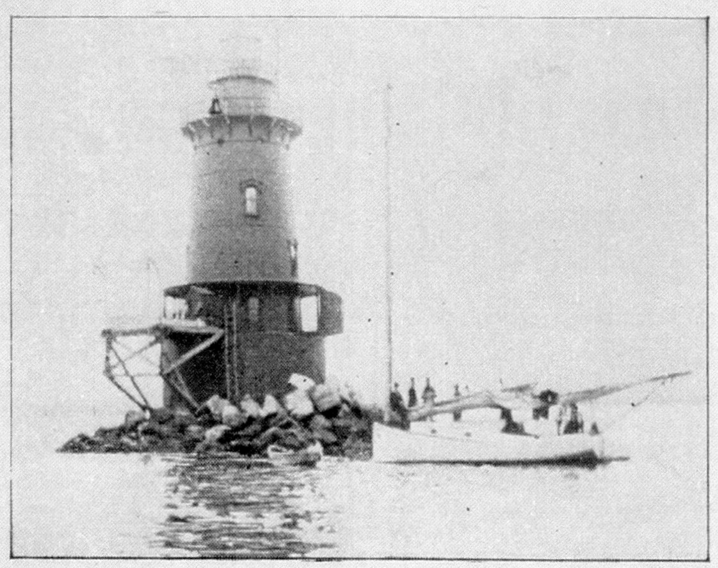

THE CONIMICUT LIGHT.

THE CONTENTS

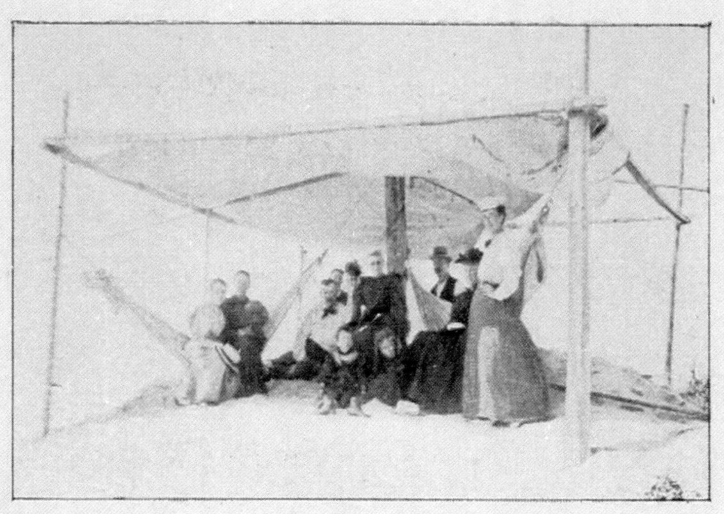

ON THE BEACH AT QUONOCONTAUG.

LIST OF ILLUSTRATIONS

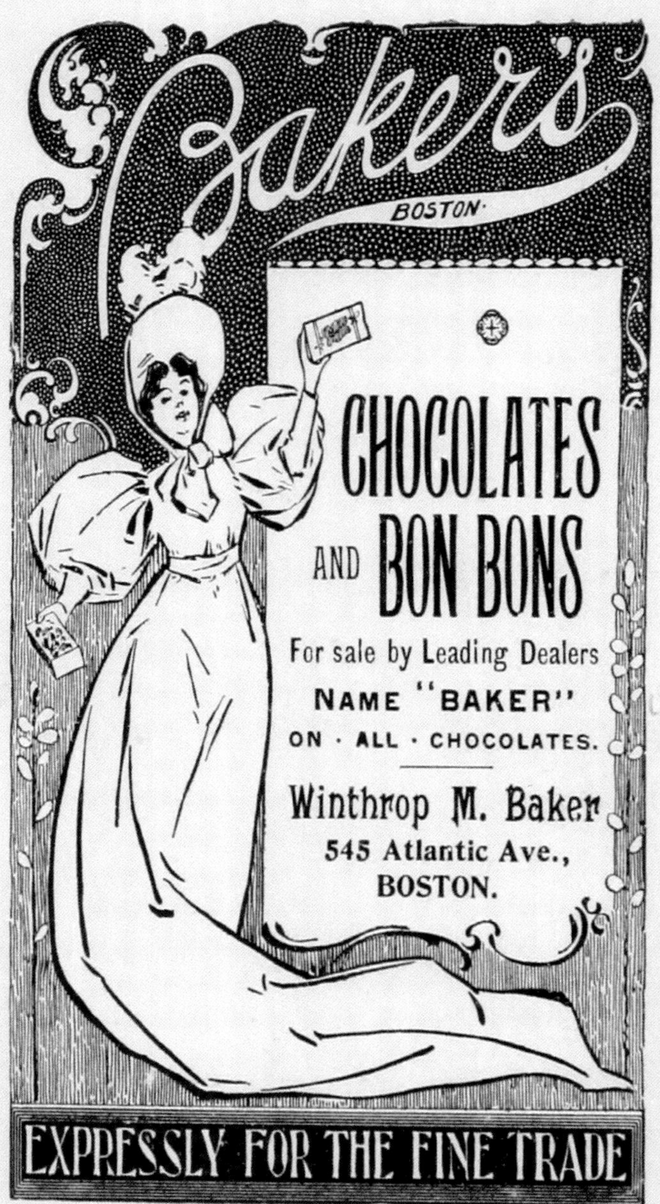
Baker's
BOSTON
CHOCOLATES
AND BON BONS
For sale by Leading Dealers
NAME "BAKER"
ON · ALL · CHOCOLATES.
Winthrop M. Baker
545 Atlantic Ave.,
BOSTON.
EXPRESSLY FOR THE FINE TRADE

LIST OF ILLUSTRATIONS—Continued.

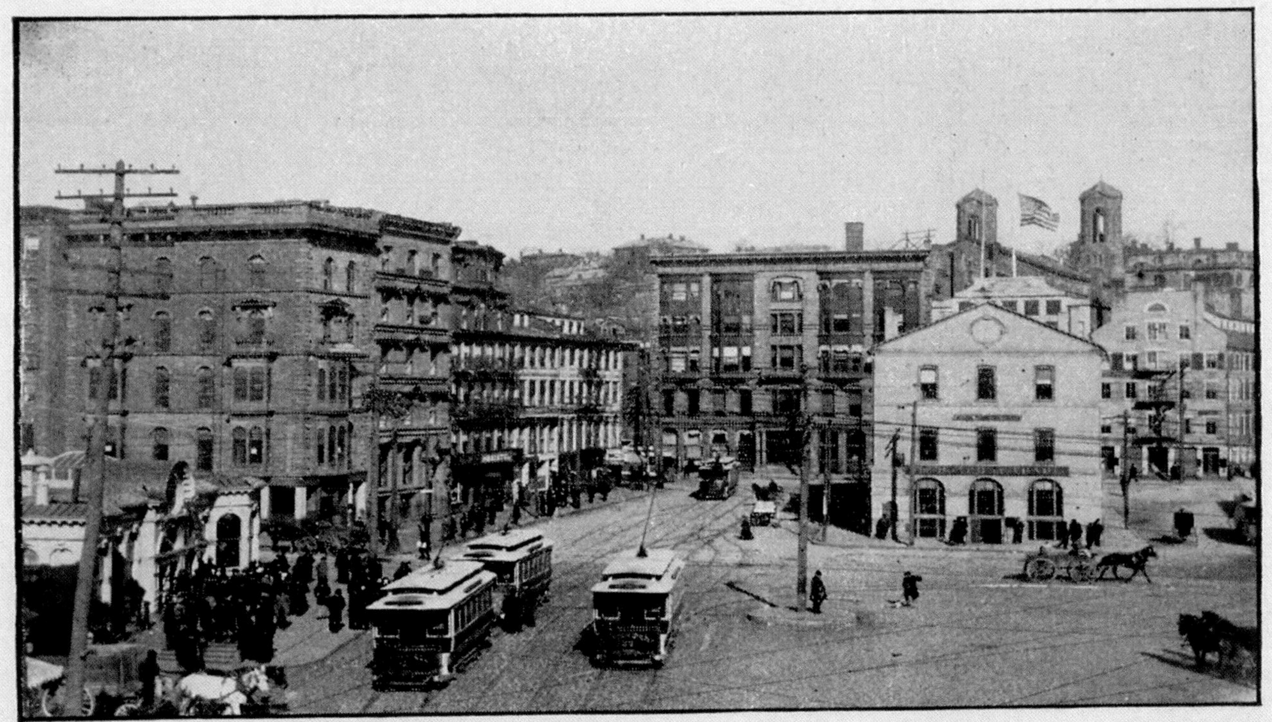

THE GREAT BRIDGE, PROVIDENCE.

Head of River and Bay.

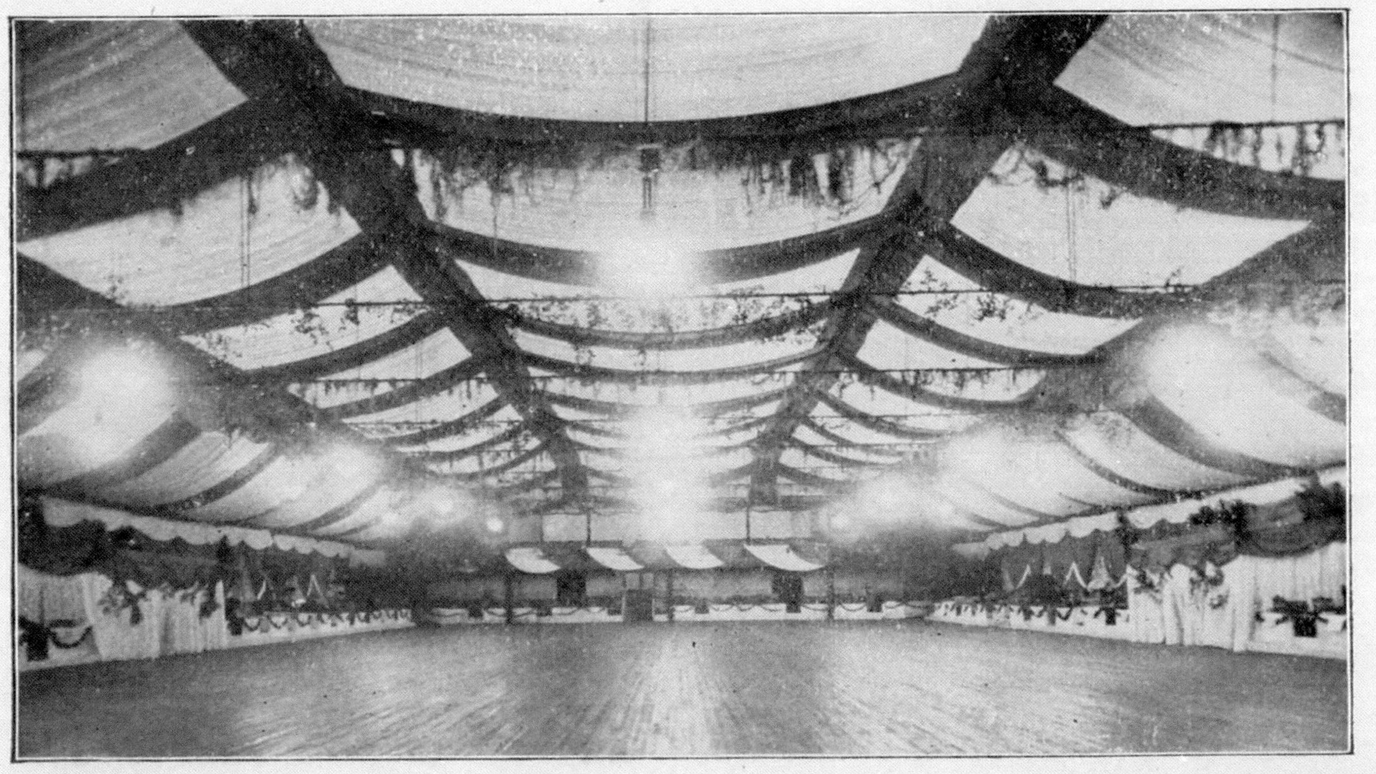

NEW HAVEN 2D REGIMENT ARMORY BY ELECTRIC LIGHT.

THE GREAT BRIDGE, PROVIDENCE

❧❧❧

❧❧❧❧PROVIDENCE, the beautiful city at the head of navigation on the Bay, is in itself a most desirable summer home. Fortunately situated upon seven hills, it has plenty of air space between for the generous circulation of the breezes which come up from the sea almost every day in the year. The homes upon the main avenues, and in the suburbs, which are readily reached by "locals" and "electrics" are made attractive by well-kept lawns and fine shade trees. ❧❧❧ The introduction of the trolley system has brought into convenient distance many desirable localities. ❧❧❧ The GREAT BRIDGE, the "electric" centre, is the converging point for all the region about Providence, and during the excursion season it presents almost a holiday appearance morning and night—especially on Sundays, the great day for down-the-river trips. ❧ Thousands of people make this their day for outings, and from this point and its immediate neighborhood, take in the parks, Field's Point, Bullock's Point, Crescent Park, Rocky Point, Newport, Seaconnet and Block Island. ❧❧❧ The cosmopolitan character of the present population of Rhode Island is well shown in the liberal patronage bestowed upon these shore caterers.

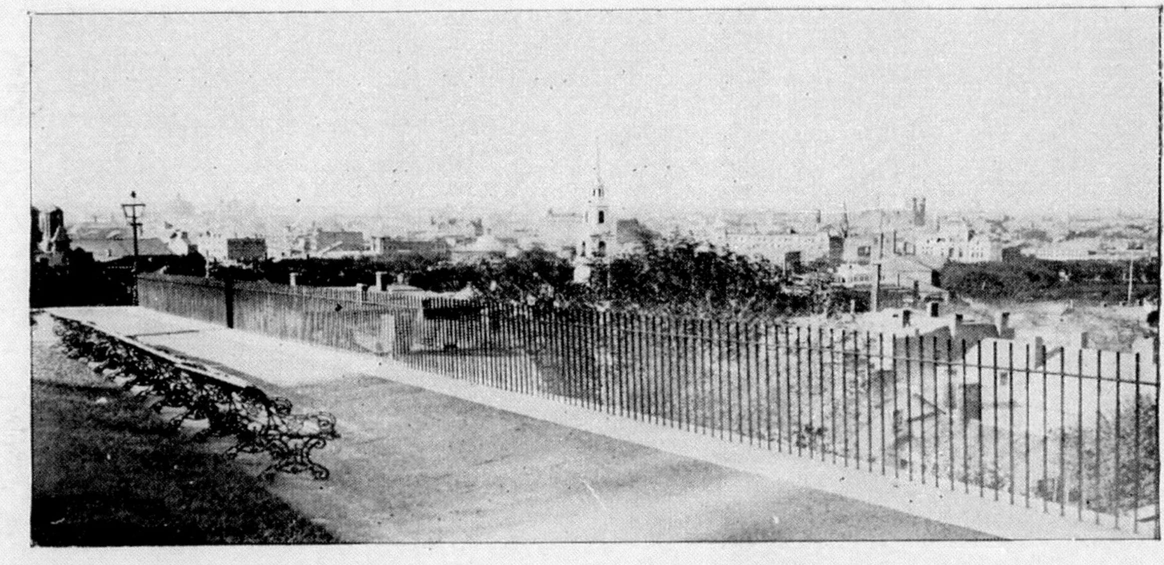

PROVIDENCE.—PROSPECT TERRACE VIEW.

Fire to Burn!

Now We Have It.

The Only Brilliant Colored Fires for
Hotels, Cottagers, and
Campers.

They Burn Brighter!

Last Longer and Cost Less

Than any other make and are
absolutely safe.

Write for Prices.

Aetna Pyrotechnic Co.

Hartford, Conn.

PROSPECT TERRACE

Prospect Terrace, from which a fine view may be had of a large portion of the City of Providence and the adjacent towns, is a short distance from the Great Bridge. The outlook is superb and well repays a trip to the top of the hill upon which it is situated. The best way to reach the Terrace is by electric car on the "Brown Street" line to Bowen street, then taking it leisurely along that pleasant thoroughfare to Congdon street, turning to the left to the little park which the city has wisely set apart as one of its pleasure grounds. The central, northwestern and southwestern sections of Providence present a pleasing sight, and in the picture will be found many of its main objects of interest: The Cathedral, the City Hall, the High School on Summer street, the Custom House, the First Baptist and Grace churches, the old Depot, the manufactories along the Woonasquatucket river, and the green hills outlined in the distant horizon. In the evening, when the city is illuminated, the view is of a different kind, fairy-like and enchanting. Should one prefer to climb the hill, take North Main, Waterman and Congdon streets on a walk. It will take about ten minutes from the Bridge.

The Merchants National Bank

PROVIDENCE, R. I.

20 WESTMINSTER STREET, GROUND FLOOR.

Abstract of Report to the Comptroller,
May 7th, 1896:

Resources.			Liabilities.		
Loans.....		$2,944,067.04	Capital.................		$1,000,000.00
U.S. Bonds, 4%.........		900,000.00	Surplus............		200,000.00
Premium U.S. Bonds..		81,500.00	Undivided Profits.....		139,561.43
Stocks and Securities..		280,047.56	National Bank Notes outstanding..........		790,000.00
Banking House........		149,334.72	DEPOSITS.		
Due from Banks other than Reserve........		96,133.40	Banks.	$925,997.02	
Checks and Cash.......		38,034.49	Individuals,	1,491,376.82	
Specie and Legals,	$148,893.39		Demand Certificates of Deposit,	500,169.50	
5% Fund.......	40,500.00				
Due from reserve banks,	368,594.17				
Total Reserve........		557,987.56	Total Deposit		2,917,543.34
		$5,047,104.77			$5,047,104.77

(Reserve Required, $416,300)

Liberal arrangements made with Depositors for Interest on Current Accounts. Interest allowed from date of deposit to date of withdrawal on Certificates of Deposit payable on demand.

ROYAL C. TAFT, President. JOHN W. VERNON, Cashier.
MOSES J. BARBER, Assistant Cashier.

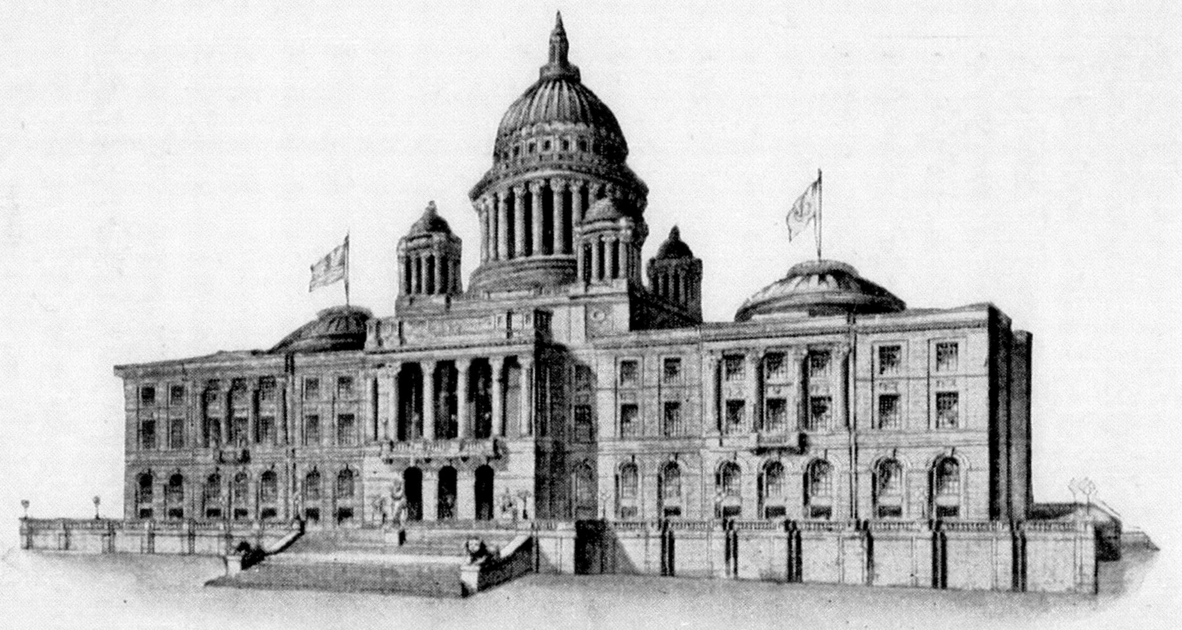

THE NEW STATE HOUSE
Providence.

THE STATE HOUSE.

☙☙☙

☙☙The new State House will be a noticeable feature during the present season.☙☙☙It is located in a conspicuous position on Smith's Hill, within a short walk of the new Union Railroad Station.☙☙The foundation was laid in the fall of 1895, and the building will be well along by the close of this year.☙☙ ☙☙The Legislature has appropriated for its erection $1,576,000.☙The Old State House on Benefit street, fronting South Main, an unpretentious three-story building, is worth a visit.☙☙It was erected in 1760, and contains many paintings and matters of historic interest.☙ The original charter of King Charles II., granted in 1663, and under which the State lived until 1843, hangs in the room of the Secretary of State.☙ Another document in the same room is the Royal Order appointing a commission to investigate the burning of the Gaspee by the Patriots in 1770.☙☙A portion of Benjamin Franklin's printing press forms one of the corner pieces of the frame of this document. ☙☙Around the walls of this room are hung many gubernatorial portraits, some of the subjects arrayed in the quaint costume of two centuries ago, while on the west side of the room is a full length portrait of George Washington, painted by Gilbert Stuart.

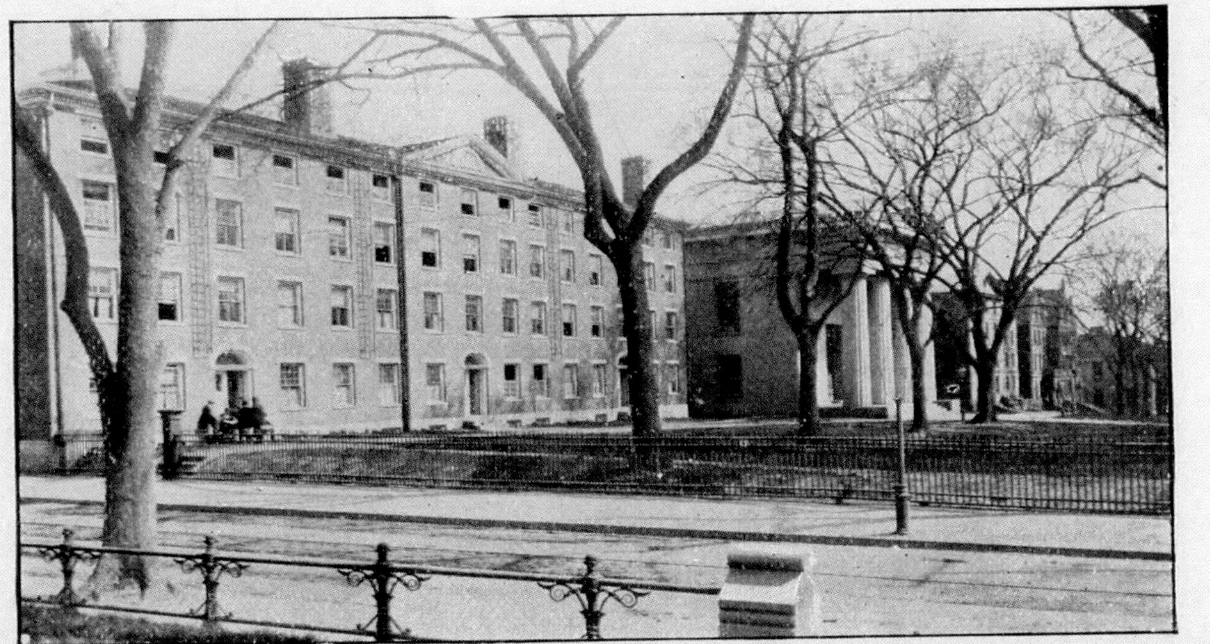

THE UNIVERSITY BUILDINGS—FRONT CAMPUS.

BROWN UNIVERSITY,

❧❧❧

❧❧❧The pride and glory of all cultivated minds in this section, occupies also a commanding position in the city as to the location of its many interesting buildings.❧The main structures front on Prospect street, and in the summer season, especially about Commencement time, their appearance and effect is heigthened by the grand old elms which make the Front Campus one of the most beautiful small bits of landscape in Providence.❧The lawns and walks are kept in excellent condition, and a stroll about the institutions is a pleasure.❧❧❧The buildings fronting on Prospect street are Hope College, Manning Hall, University Hall, Slater Hall, Rhode Island Hall, the Library on the corner of Prospect and Waterman streets, and the home of the President, Dr. E. B. Andrews, corner of College and Prospect streets.❧❧❧Fronting on the Back Campus are the Chemical Laboratory, the Gymnaseum, the Machine Shop, the Heating Station, Sayles Memorial Hall, (in which are fine portraits of a number of distinguished men of Rhode Island), Wilson Hall, and Maxey Hall.❧❧The new Dormatory for Women will be located corner Brown and Cushing streets in the near neighborhood, and the

BROWN UNIVERSITY.—Continued.

Ladd Observatory is on Observatory street, between East avenue and Olney street. ☙The janitor of the University will show visitors about the buildings at all reasonable times. ☙☙☙Lincoln Field, the scene of the base-ball and foot-ball triumphs, fronts on Thayer street, in the rear of the University buildings. ☙☙Next the Library, on Waterman street, is the Cabinet of the Rhode Island Historical Society. ☙The easiest means of access to these places is by way of the electric lines over College Hill. ☙☙☙Among the other educational institutions in Providence which have helped to make its enviable reputation as a seat of learning, THE FRIENDS SCHOOL, on Hope, near Olney street, is one of the oldest and best. ☙☙☙It was established in 1784 by the Friends — but its halls are open to the youth of all denominations and of both sexes. ☙The PROVIDENCE BRYANT & STRATTON BUSINESS COLLEGE, whose home is in the Hoppin Homestead Building, 357 Westminster street, ranks with the leading commercial schools of the country. It is doing a great work in the community in training the youth of both sexes for positions of trust and responsibility. ☙☙☙☙

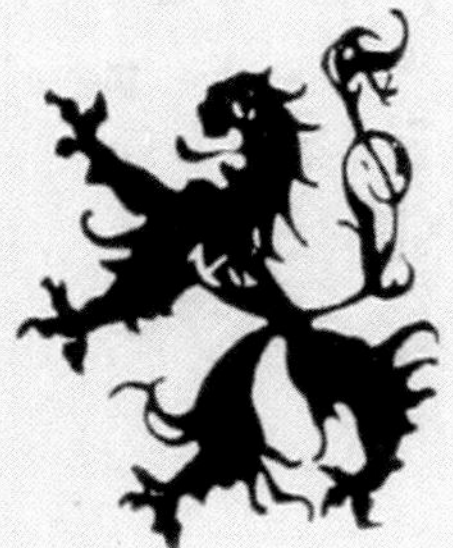

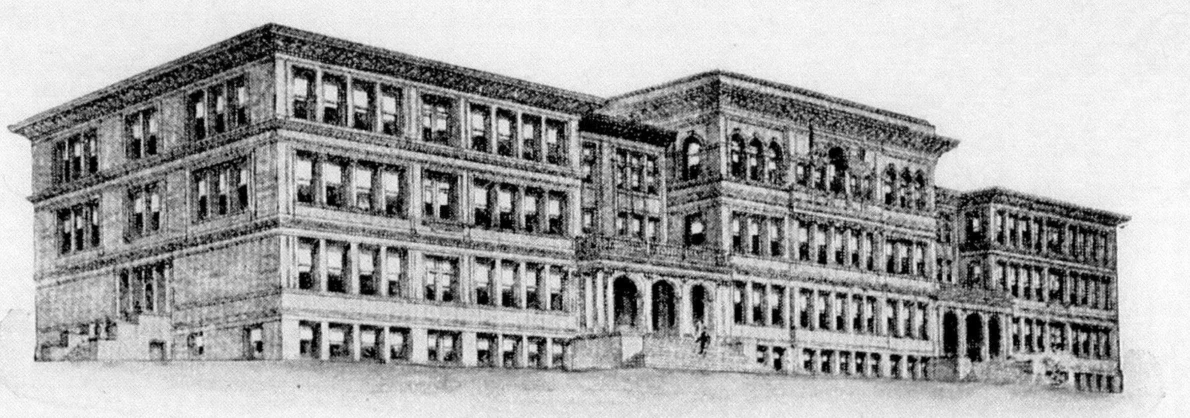

THE STATE NORMAL SCHOOL

Lincoln and Park Streets.

THE STATE NORMAL SCHOOL

❧❧❧

❧❧❧One of the most important of the educational institutions of Providence is the State Normal School, at the corner of Benefit and Waterman streets.❧It was established in 1851 as a preparatory school for Brown University and to fit pupils for teaching. It became a city institution early in 1854, and later in the same year the State assumed control of it.❧ The building now used—a substantial three-story structure—was built in 1843 for the Providence High School, and assumed its present functions in 1879, after the completion of the present High School building on Summer street.❧The Normal School, in its turn, has outgrown the building, and a new and commodious structure, at the corner of Park and Lincoln streets, not far from the new State House, is now in process of erection.❧The State appropriated $250,000 for the purpose.❧It will contain accommodations for a training school, embracing kindergarten, primary and grammar school training departments, and for all the courses of the normal grade.❧❧This school is an indispensable adjunct of the educational system of the State.❧❧About 68 per cent. of those graduated during the past ten years are still teaching.❧In its new home its influence will be extended.

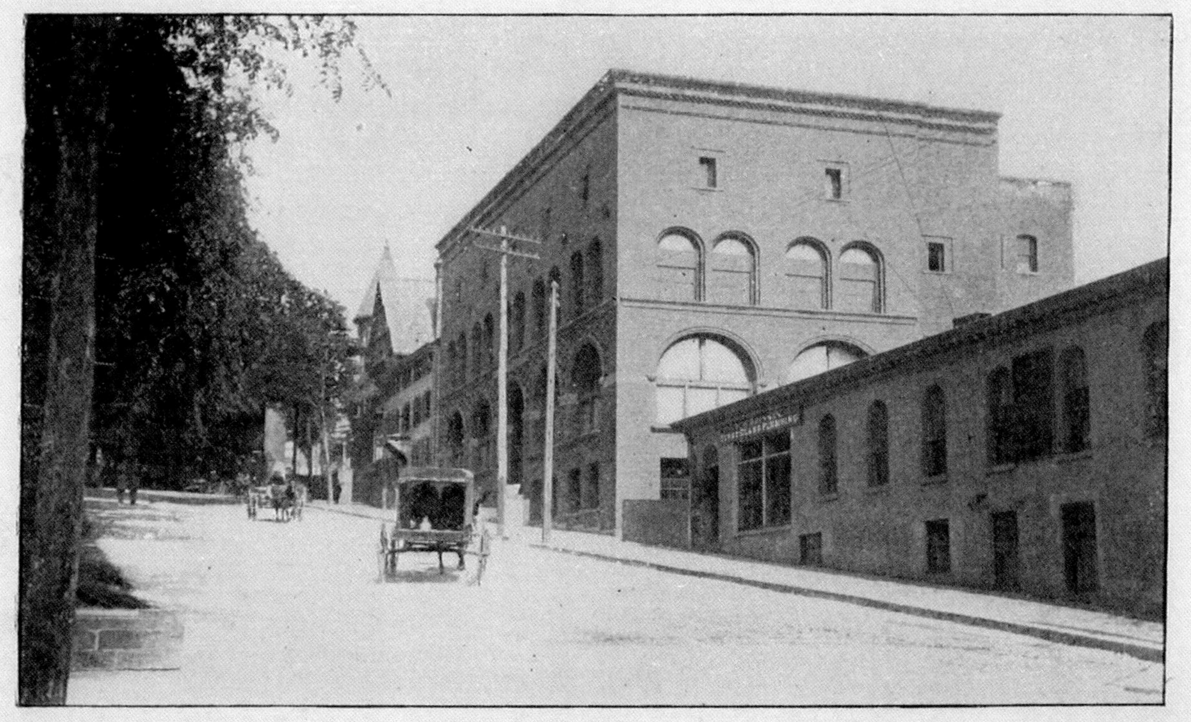

WATERMAN STREET AND SCHOOL OF DESIGN.

THE SCHOOL OF DESIGN,

❧ ❧ ❧

❧❧❧One of the most useful and best equipped training and artistic schools in the city, is situated on Waterman, near North Main street.❧❧❧The school was originally established through the devotion and personal efforts of the late Mrs. Jesse Metcalf.❧❧❧Through the munificence of her self and husband the fine edifice which now affords opportunity for the development and encouragement of the taste, skill and ingenuity of Rhode Island youth, was erected.❧❧The purposes of the institution are the instruction of artisans in decorating, painting, modeling and drawing; "the systematic training of students in the practice of art," and the general advancement of art education by the exhibition of works of art and art studies, and by lectures on art.❧❧The Museum is open free to the public from 2 to 5 p. m. (Sundays included.)❧❧❧ THE ART CLUB, with its home at 11 Thomas street, nearly opposite the School of Design, is composed of the leaders in art matters in the community, and at various seasons gives exhibitions in its gallery which are of general public interest.❧❧❧❧It has done good work in developing and centralizing effort in this field.❧❧❧

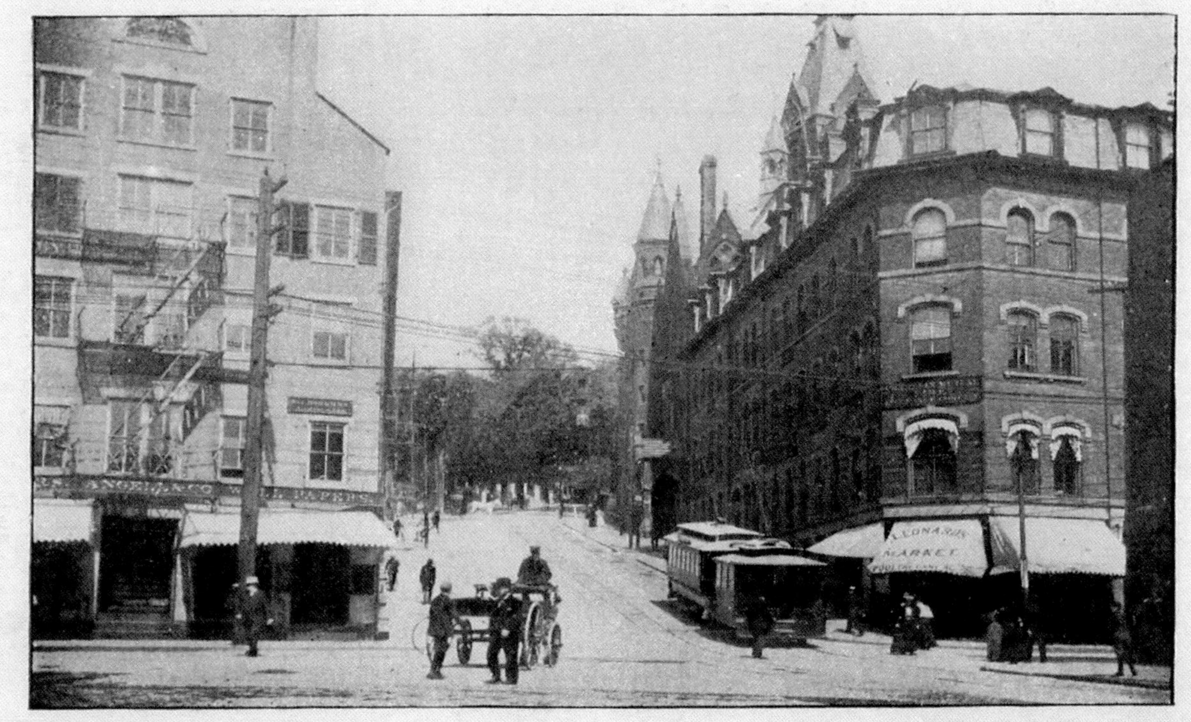

COLLEGE STREET AND THE COURT HOUSE.

OVER COLLEGE HILL.

☙☙☙

☙☙☙The trips by the electrics over College Hill are varied and delightful.☙They take one through a fine section of the East side.☙The Court House, corner of Benefit and College streets, and the Athenaeum, opposite, are noteworthy buildings, and the Talma Theatre — to be located a few doors north on Benefit street — will complete a trio of interest in the near future.☙For a ride to the Resevoir and that region take the Brown street car.☙To Blackstone Park and to connect with a 'bus for Swan Point, the Elmwood and Broadway lines.☙For Phillipsdale a pleasant country district, the Phillipsdale line.☙To Daisyfield, Rumford, East Providence Centre, Hunt's Mills and one of the pleasantest of rural districts, take the Rumford car.☙To the Seekonk river — along which the city will soon have completed a fine driveway — the regular Olneyville, Angell street and Broadway cars.☙The Angell street cars all pass the Central Church, one of the newer and most ornate additions to the places of worship in the city.☙The introduction of the cable, and later the electric lines, through this portion of Providence and its eastern suburbs has made available for homes a large and beautiful district.

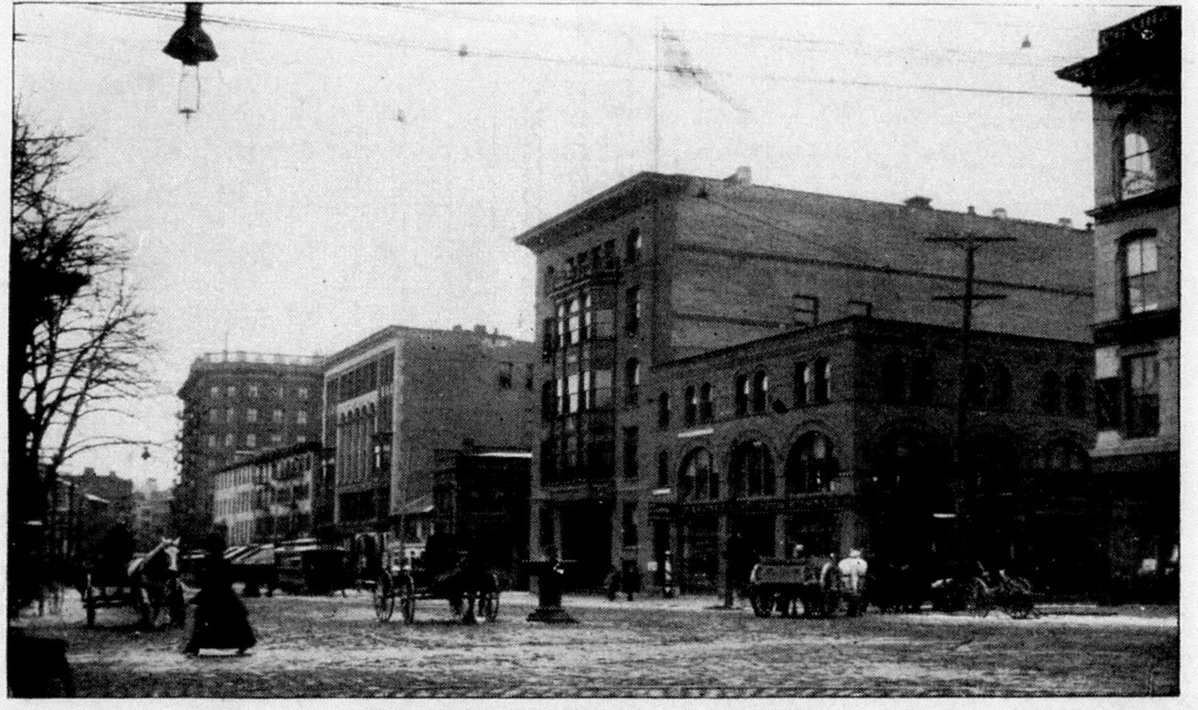

WEYBOSSET STREET

Narragansett Hotel — Flint's — Hodges Bld'g — Wirth's — Athletic Club — Wm. Sweeney's — C. S. Bush Co.

WEYBOSSET STREET.

❧❧❧

❧❧❧The improvements on Weybosset street in its architectural features within the last few years have been notable.❧The Post Office, the Narragansett Hotel, "Flints," the City Hotel, and the "Round Top" Church, are old landmarks.❧The addition of the Studley, Swarts, Hodges, Fletcher, The Athletic Club, and the Anthony & Cowell buildings have materially changed the face of the street for the better, and the impetus given will tell for further improvements in the near future.❧The best way to see this thoroughfare is to take one of the electrics of the Broad street route to Pawtuxet.❧After passing the "Round Top" Church the principal notable buildings are the New Convent, the Union Congregational, Trinity Methodist Episcopal, and the New Church, and the Home for Aged Men, at the corner of Broad and Laura streets.❧The rest of the route is through a pleasant residence section passing the eastern entrance to Roger Williams Park, Washington Park, Edgewood, and reaching the terminus at Pawtuxet, where a sight of the quaint little homes in the older section, and the beautiful modern cottages on the Neck, well repays the slight expense of time and money the trip costs.

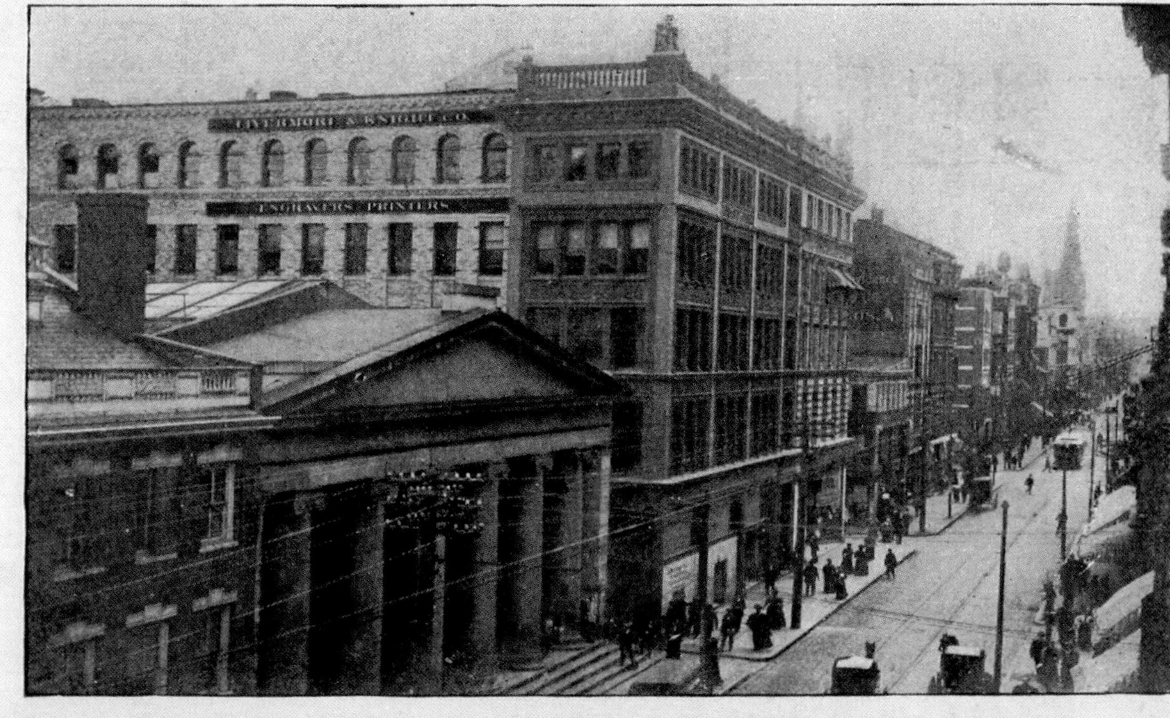

THE ARCADE AND WESTMINSTER STREET.

Looking Westward.

Facial Defects

Nothing is more Repulsive

and disgusting than

DECAYED, FOUL AND

DISCOLORED ☘ TEETH

These Defects are removed in the most satisfactory and painless manner by ☘

DR. WILLIAMS, In the HOYLE BUILDING.

☘☘☘☘☘☘☘☘☘☘☘☘☘☘☘

He also manufactures the most sure and reliable

CATARRH ☘ CURE

Known. ☘☘☘☘☘ It gives relief at once.
Trial Bottle, 10c. Large Bottle, 50c.
Call at his Office,

874 Westminster Street

Room No. 1

Providence, R. I.

WESTMINSTER STREET.

❧❧❧The finest business thoroughfare in the metropolis of Rhode Island, traverses the city from east to west.❧❧From the Great Bridge to Olneyville Square, its terminus, the distance is about two miles. Taking the green car at the Bridge, and using the eye of observation, many fine buildings will be noticed, principal among them at the start, the striking granite structure of The Rhode Island Hospital Trust Company, the Merchants Bank building, the Industrial Trust Company's new banking house, "The Banigan" building, and along the way the Arcade, the Butler Exchange, the Lauderdale and Francis blocks, "Kennedy's," "Barnaby's," "The Boston Store," "Shepard's," Tilden & Thurber's, and "Gladding's," Grace Church, Music Hall, the Home of the Young Men's Christain Association, the monument to the late Mayor Doyle, the Cathedral, the Union Club, All Saints and Roger Williams churches.❧After passing the junction of Weybosset and Westminster streets, the business blocks are not pretentious, but at the end of the route the evidences of ambitious thrift are shown in a number of fine places built by the merchants of the locality—San Souci Bros., and others.❧On the ride back take the blue electric of the Broadway line.

THE NEW CONVENT,

☘☘☘At the corner of Broad, Claverick and Foster streets, is one of the new and notable additions to the educational institutions of Providence.☘☘For many years the old St. Xavier's Convent of Mercy had occupied this spot, doing a quiet and efficient work in the community.☘The increasing demands upon its good offices necessitated better accommodations, and through the untiring industry of the Sisters and the liberality of many friends the commodious structure now about completed will give ample facilities for carrying on the beneficent work ot education and charity.☘ST. JOSEPH'S HOSPITAL, corner of Broad, Peace and Plenty streets, and the ST. MARIA WORKING GIRLS' HOME, 119 Govenor street, two institutions recently established and endowed for humane work, have also noticeable structures which are easily reached by the electrics of the Broad and Govenor street lines.☘☘The SS. PETER and PAUL'S CATHEDRAL, corner of Westminster and Fenner streets—one of the grandest church edifices in New England, — and the institutions noted above, express in a way the best hopes, aspirations, and desires of a large portion of the community, and show how closely the interests of all are interwoven.☘☘

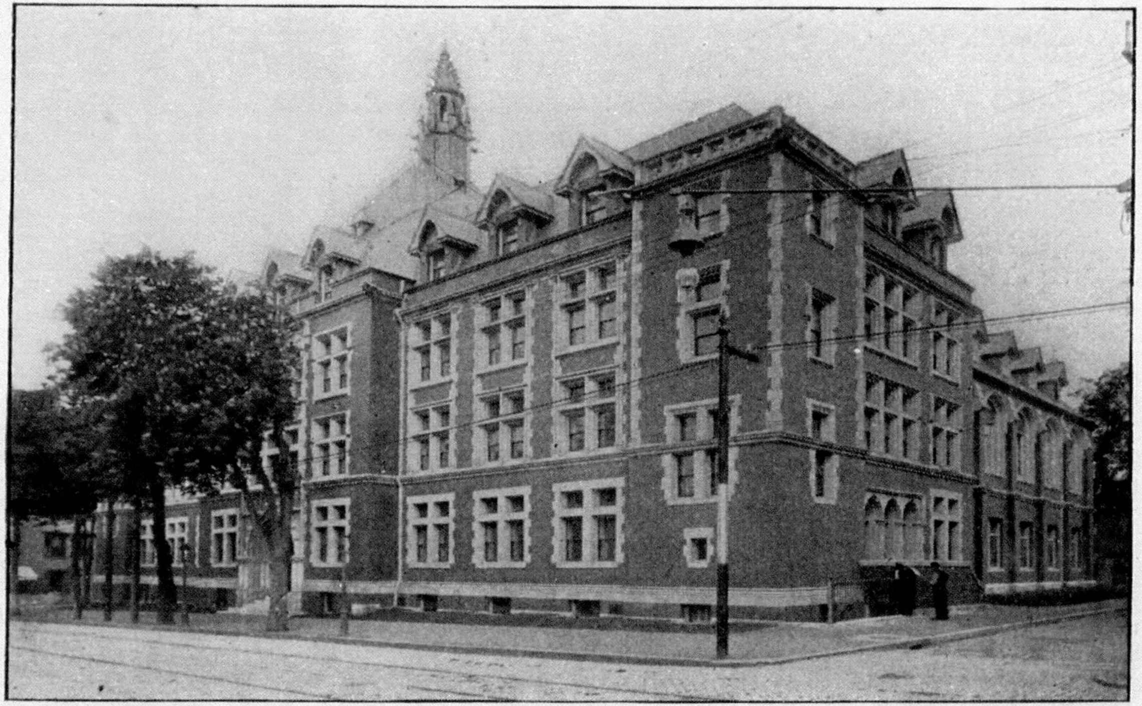

THE NEW ST. FRANCIS XAVIER CONVENT.

ROGER WILLIAMS PARK.

The largest, most attractive, and best known of the city's public grounds is about thirty minutes' ride from the Great Bridge. The Elmwood and Auburn cars take one over the better route to the Park, but the Broad street line also gives glimpses of pleasant sections and is a good second choice. Betsey Williams, with a generous spirit transmitted from her great ancestor, Roger Williams, gave to the city the nucleus of this beautiful outing-spot, and the Park Commissioners, with excellent taste and judgment, are extending and embellishing it for the benefit of the increasing population of Providence and suburbs. In the summer season the Park is visited daily by throngs of visitors and on Sundays it is the objective point for all the crowds that can be accommodated by the Traction Company's cars, by carriage and bicycle. Among the many points of interest the Betsey Williams House itself is a quaint and noticeable one, and remains a memorial to the founder of the Park. Located near, is the fine monument to the founder of the State—and age and familiarity with it only tends to increase admiration for its figure of History and the simple bronze statue of Roger Williams.

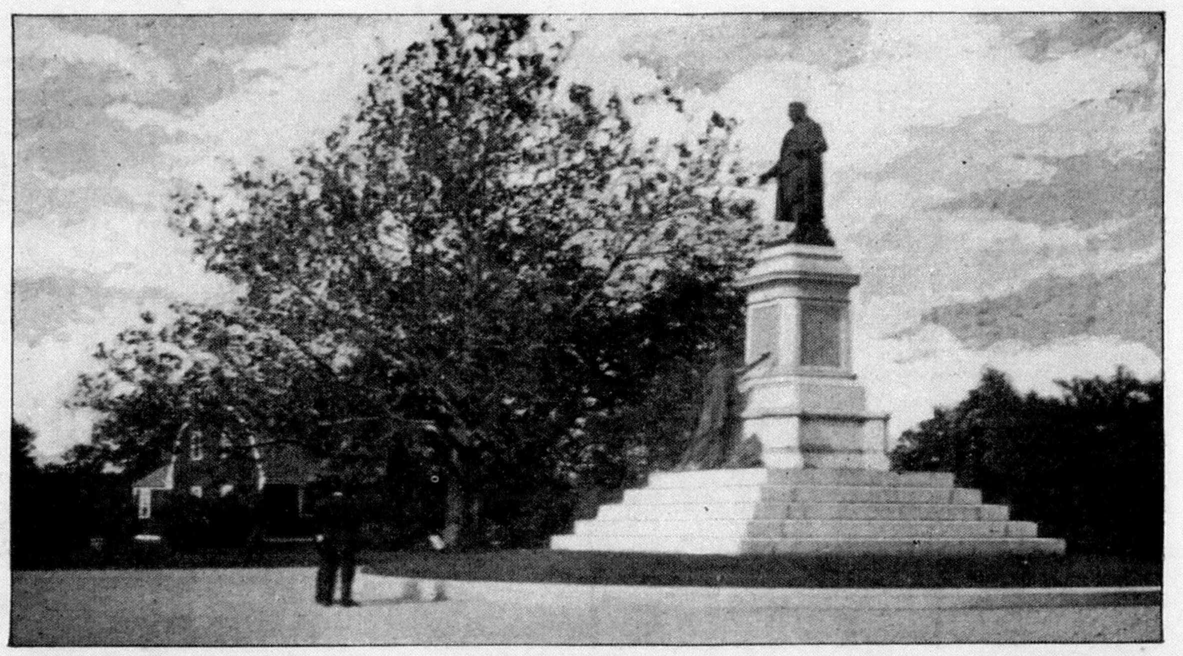

THE PARK

The Betsy Williams Cottage. The Founder's Statue, Roger Williams.

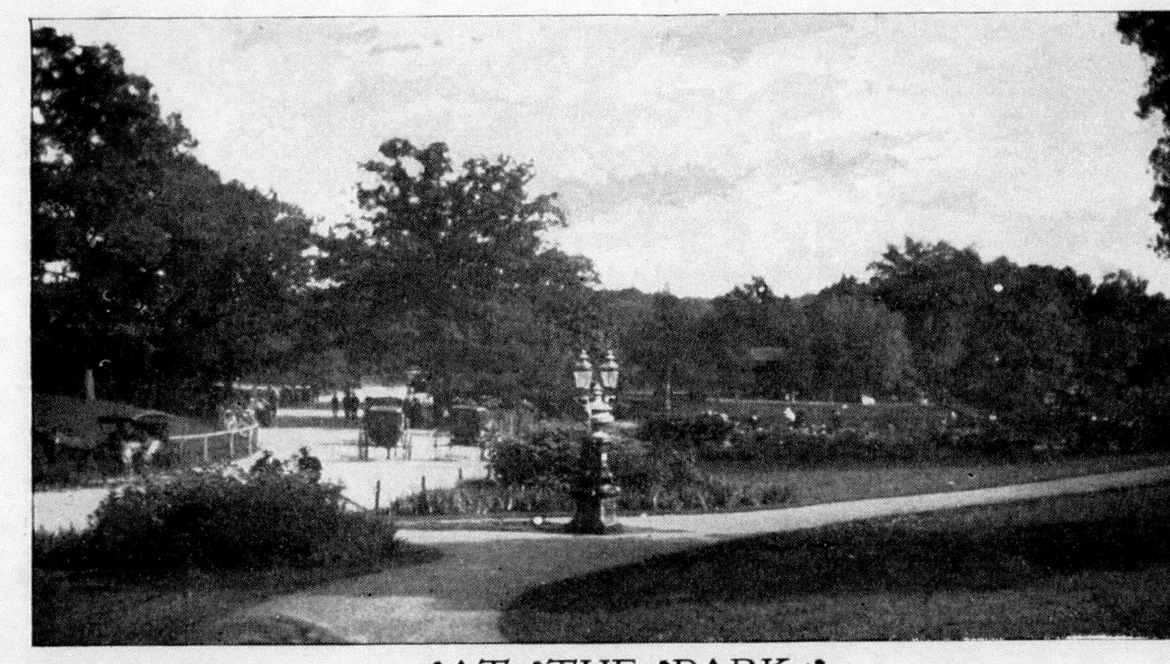

AT THE PARK

The Dalrymple Fountain and The Drive

ROGER WILLIAMS PARK.

☙☙☙

☙☙☙The old well, with its long reach, is a short distance from the little red gambrel-roofed house in which Betsey Williams lived many years, and a drink from it will be refreshing.☙☙Then a stroll about the Lake, a stop at the Cafe for a lunch or an ice cream, a rest on one of the benches near the edge of the lakes to watch the pleasure parties skimming the waters in the dainty row-boats or the gay little steam launches, or to feed the water-fowl, will serve to pass very agreeably the first hour at the Park.☙☙The DALRYMPLE FOUNTAIN and the views of the driveways near will engage attention for a moment; the memorial to the late Governor Elisha Dyer will merit a visit; the swings near the boat-house will be occupied by the little ones for a short time.☙Then a row over the Lake, or one can step into a launch and take the trip leisurely under the guidance of an efficient captain furnished by the Superintendent of the Park.☙☙A half-hour can be spent on the water with pleasure, and a return made to land with a desire to "do" the remainder of the Park with a keener zest.☙☙ Annually, on Arbor Day, the school-children help put out the trees which add to the welcome shade.

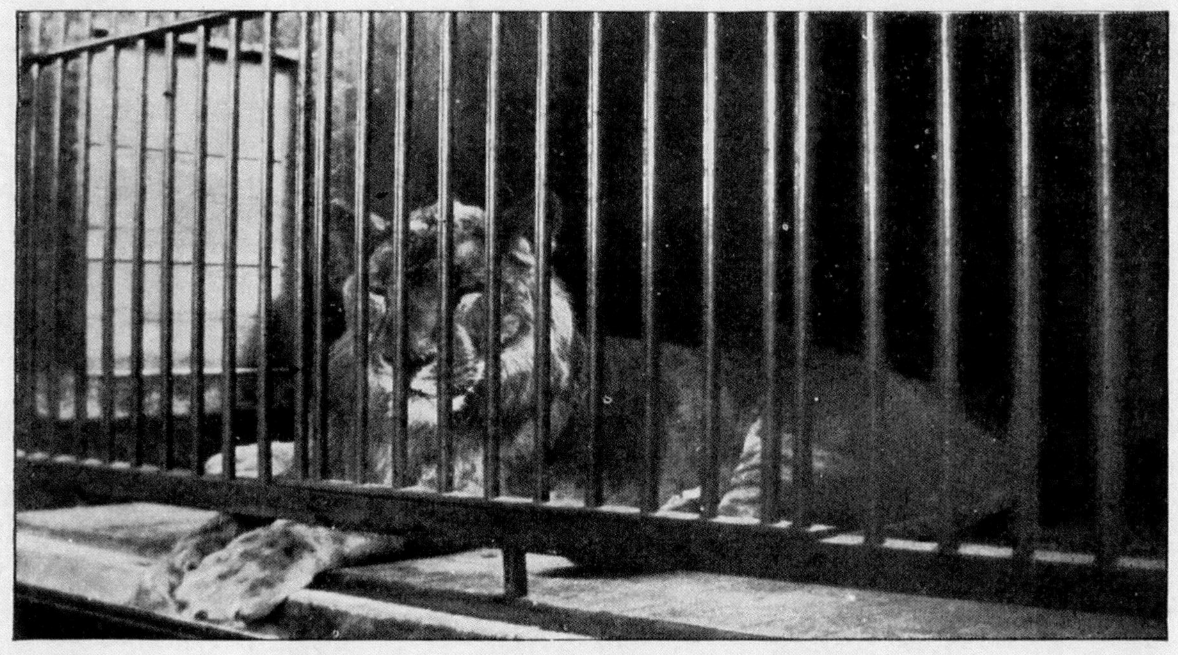

"PALM" The King of Beasts

❧❧The Menagerie and the Deer Park are always the centres of attraction.❧❧Young and old find something to amuse, admire or condemn.❧Visit after visit can be made without exhausting the subject of animal life.❧❧❧The collection is not a large, but an excellent one, and Superintendent J. B. Hathaway, who has direct personal charge, exercises the best of care and judgment in training his proteges and presenting them to the visitors in fine condition.❧❧The magnificent lion, Palm, is monarch, with his mate making a regal pair.❧The tigress, a splendid specimen of the African jungles, divides with them the admiration of all visitors.❧ The leopards, black leopards, bears, hyenas, pumas, opossums, the monkeys, Rachael, the camel, and the birds all receive great attention.❧Baby Roger—the special friend of the children—is a rapidly growing fellow, and can be seen on the green at most all times surrounded by an amused group of little folks.❧❧The prairie dogs, rabbits, eagles, and owls are not far away, and ought all to be seen.❧ ❧The New Museum Building will add another entertaining and instructive feature to the attractions of the grounds.❧❧The great bison, which recently died, and the tiger, strangled by his mate a short time since, will form the nucleus of a collection here.

PROVIDENCE RIVER.

❧❧❧

❧❧❧The wharves about the head of the river are teeming with life during the summer season.❧Excursionists come to the shores of the Bay from all parts of New England, and especially from "around about" for a distance of fifty to seventy-five miles. Societies, military organizations, Sunday schools, and made-up parties are all interested in the natural beauties of the many resorts bordering upon the Bay, and "love" the succulent clam which has made the Narragansett waters famous all over the country.❧ From the landing places on the east and west sides the boats may be taken to Field's Point, Silver Spring, Crescent Park, Rocky Point, Conanicut Park, Newport, Block Island, Bristol, Bristol Ferry, Fall River, Tiverton, and Seaconnet Point.❧The lines to all these places are admirably managed, and hundreds of thousands of people are transported annually with almost absolute safety.❧❧The excursion rates made for the summer traveler are so moderate that the pleasures of a river sail are within the limits of the closest purse.❧The sail to Newport and back, the finest of all, costs but 75 cents for the round trip.❧The Block Island round trip costs $1.00, and that to Seaconnet Point and back but 75 cents.

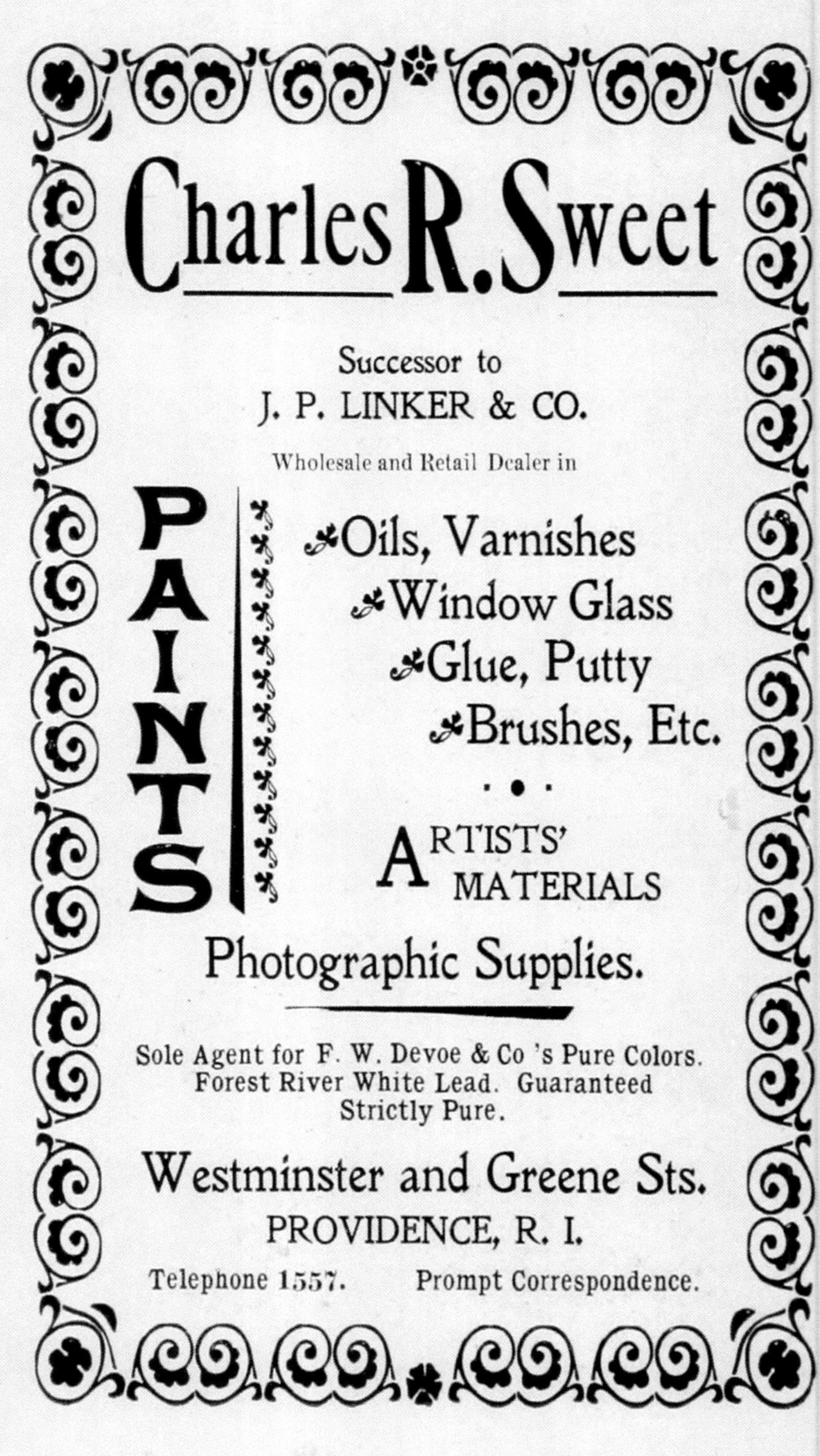
Charles R. Sweet
Successor to
J. P. LINKER & CO.
Wholesale and Retail Dealer in
PAINTS
Oils, Varnishes
Window Glass
Glue, Putty
Brushes, Etc.
ARTISTS' MATERIALS
Photographic Supplies.
Sole Agent for F. W. Devoe & Co 's Pure Colors.
Forest River White Lead. Guaranteed
Strictly Pure.
Westminster and Greene Sts.
PROVIDENCE, R. I.
Telephone 1557.
Prompt Correspondence.

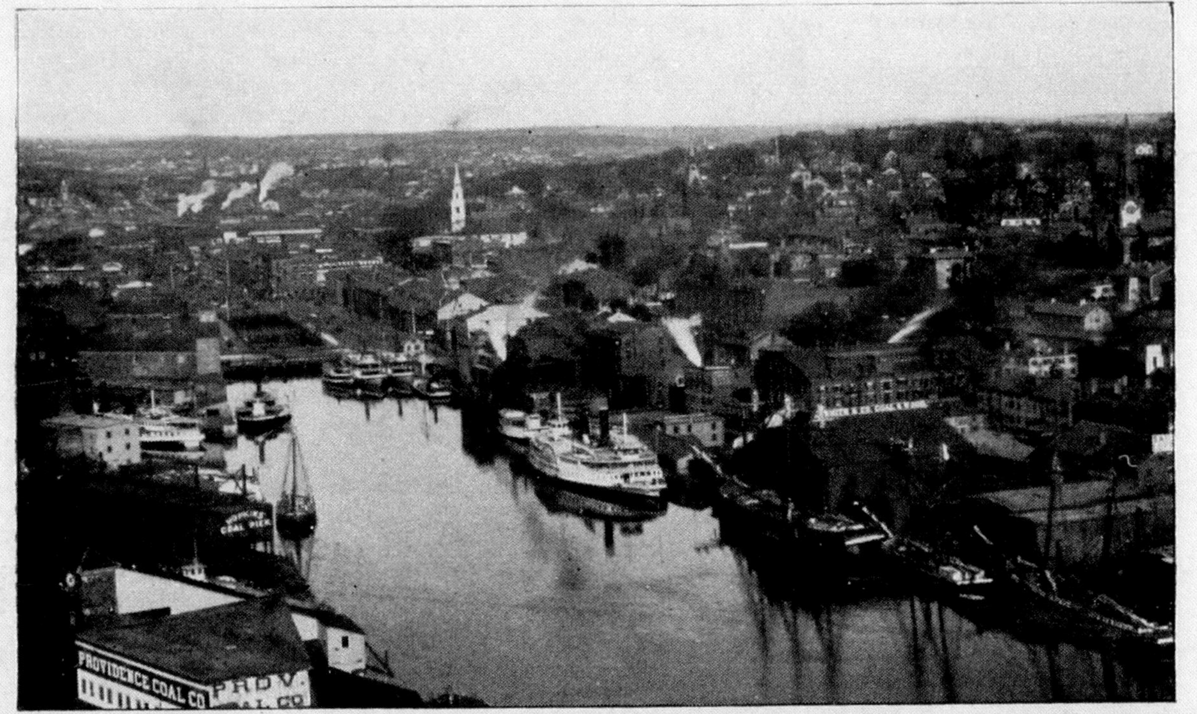

PROVIDENCE RIVER AND THE EAST SIDE

Newport Boats — First Baptist Spire — East Side
Providence Coal Co. — Seaconnet Boats — Fall River Boats

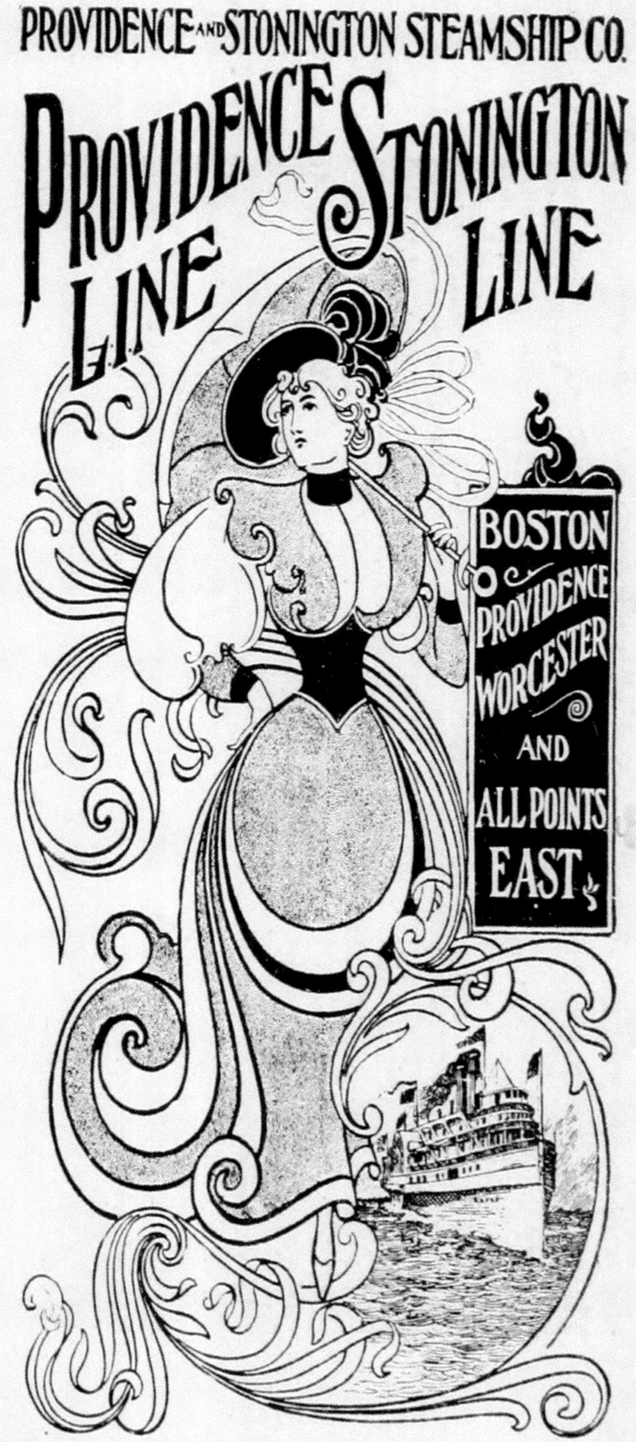

PROVIDENCE AND STONINGTON STEAMSHIP CO.

PROVIDENCE LINE

STONINGTON LINE

BOSTON
PROVIDENCE
PROVIDENCE
WORCESTER
AND
ALL POINTS
EAST

J. W. MILLER,	GEO. L. CONNOR,	W. DeW. DIMOCK,	O. H. BRIGGS,
President.	Pass'r Traffic Mgr.	Asst. Gen'l Pass'r Agt.	Gen'l Pass'r Agt.

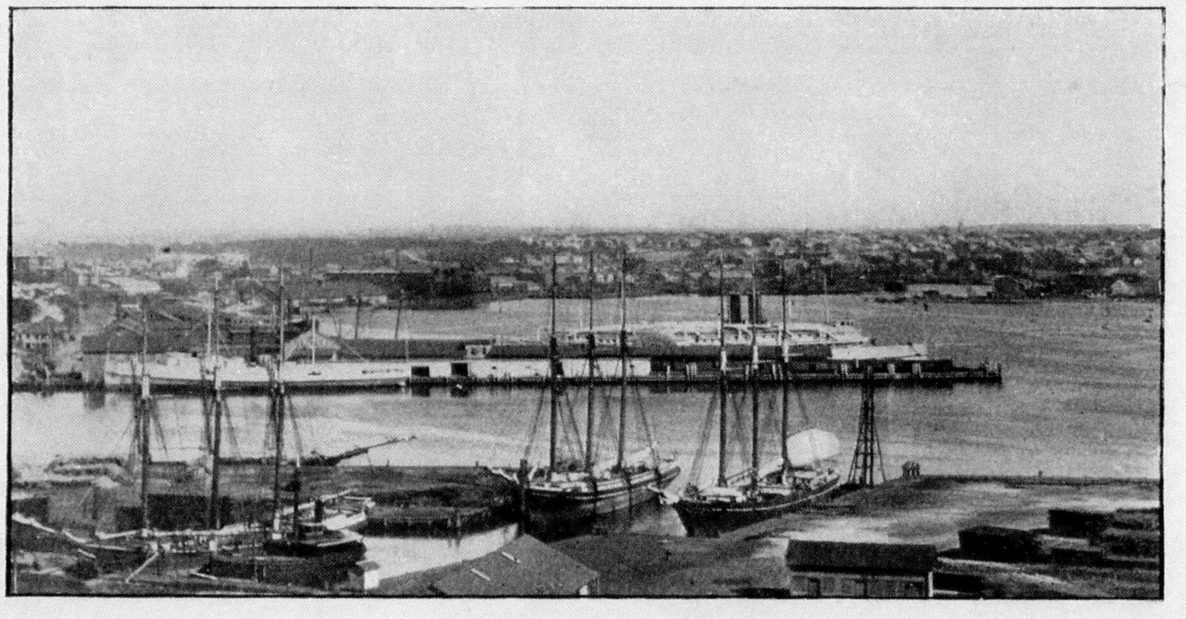

FOX POINT, PROVIDENCE.

Starting Point of the Providence Line Steamers. East Providence in the Distance.

FOX POINT.

☙☙☙

☙☙☙The sail from Providence to New York by one of the magnificent steamers of the Providence Line is a never-to-be-forgotten pleasure.☙Leaving Fox Point Wharf at 7.45 o'clock of a summer evening one has a panoramic view of land and water which is scarcely exceeded in beauty even by that of the Hudson River.☙The shores of the Bay for a long distance are covered with the homes of cottagers, and when the evenings have grown long the pyrotechnical displays from both shores give a romantic "send off" to the beginning of the trip through Providence River.☙The steamers "Massachusetts" and "Connecticut," which will make the voyages this season, are two of the best representatives of modern skill in structure and equipment sailing in American waters.☙The search-light of the "Connecticut" illumines the way, affords additional safety by denoting the position of other craft, aids the traveler to make out the coast line, and salutes in return the places along the shore.☙☙ The trips to New York are made every day except Sundays.☙☙☙The Stonington Line for New York can be taken at all times during the year, from the Union Depot, (Sunday excepted) at 7.05 and 8 P. M.

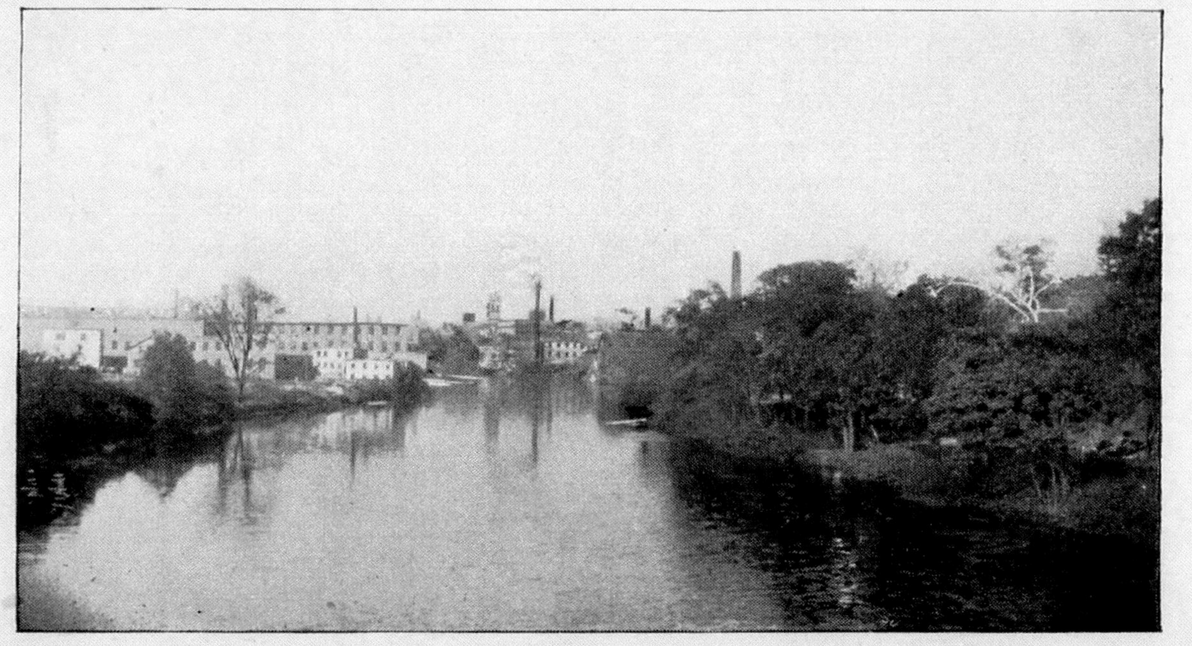

BLACKSTONE RIVER AT PAWTUCKET

❧ PAWTUCKET. ❧

❧ The second city of importance in Rhode Island, and equaling in enterprise and ambition the first, Pawtucket, at the head of the Seekonk river, should be "taken in" by all visitors who have more than a day to spend about the shores and headwaters of Narragansett Bay. ❧ ❧ ❧ The busy manufacturing establishments, and the many new buildings on its main streets, give evidence of the faith and ability of her business men — the pleasant homes, of their taste and thrift. ❧ ❧ Conant's Thread Mills, "Goff's Braid" Mills, the Pawtucket Hair Cloth Works, the Union Wadding Company — concerns with world-wide reputations — and many others almost equally famous are located here, giving employment to thousands of skilled workers, and adding renown and wealth to this thriving city. ❧ ❧ ❧ The merchants, though so close to the competition of Providence, exhibit the pluck and energy, in the erection of fine buildings, which keeps the old trade and attracts new. "The New Idea Store"—Shartenburg & Robinson's — the Boston Store, the New England Store, Carpenter & Company's, and the Boston & Providence Clothing Company's, are stores of the up-to-date character which have helped to make the modern Pawtucket a city well worth knowing. ❧

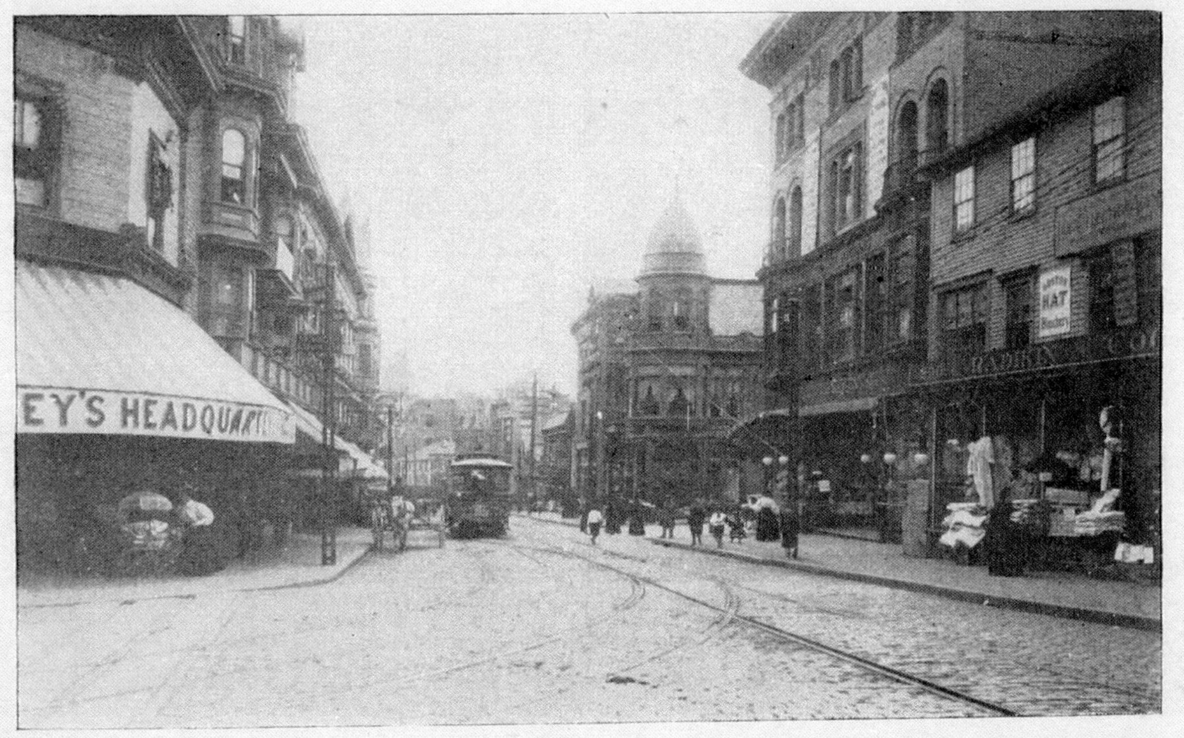

MAIN STREET, PAWTUCKET.

MAIN STREET, PAWTUCKET.

❧❧The principal retail thoroughfare in Pawtucket is rather unfortunate in formation and does not do justice to the city as a representative street.❧❧The fine buildings which are being erected for the transaction of the rapidly increasing local traffic will in a great degree, however, compensate in beauty for the lack of evenness and correctness of outline in the street.❧❧Within the last few years the spirit of improvement has been making many changes in and around Main street, and the metropolitan instinct which fosters everything to encourage the trade at home has found expression in more tasteful blocks and inviting stores.❧The displays of goods are made as tempting as in the neighboring city, and merchandise sold at as reasonable a price. ❧❧The Music Hall building, the Pacific National Bank building, on this street, the Kinyon, Taylor and Smith blocks, and the new home of the Times newspaper, on connecting streets, are attractive business additions which mark the progressive era of the new Pawtucket.❧❧The addition of the new retail blocks has been well supplimented by the extension of the manufacturing industries, and with an improved general business throughout the country, a prosperous future is in store for this pushing city. ❧

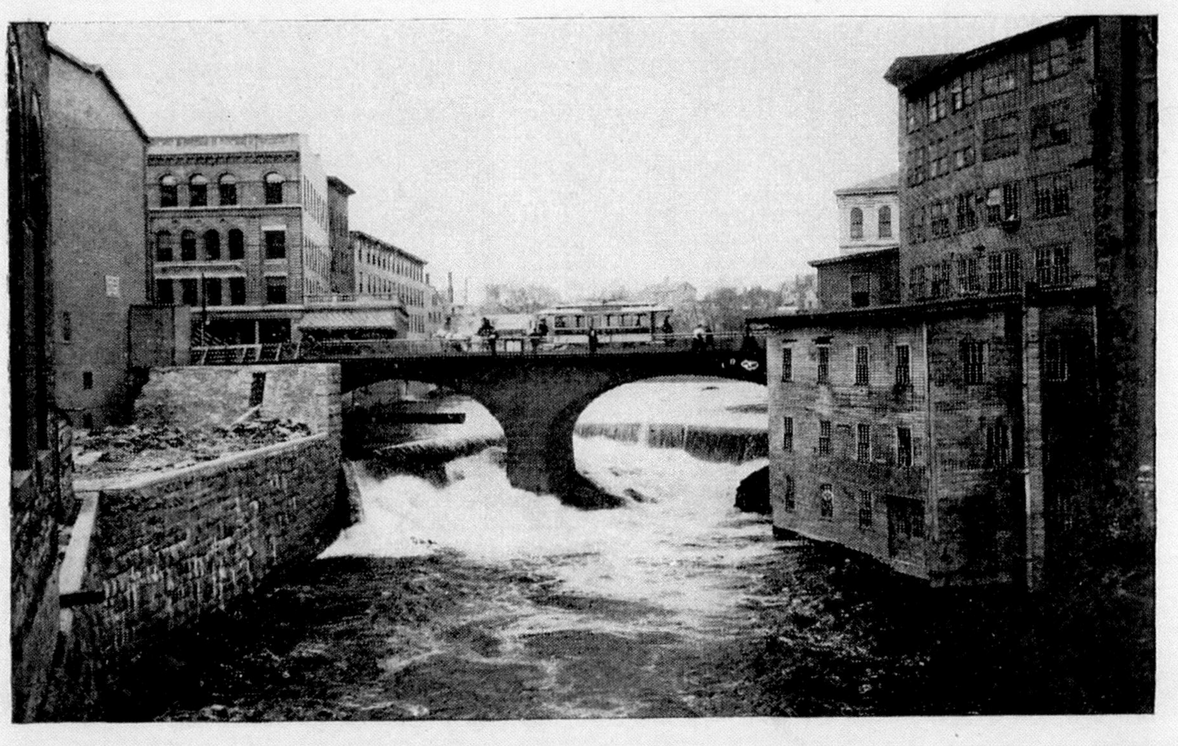

THE FALLS, PAWTUCKET.

☙ THE FALLS. ☙

☙ ☙ ☙

☙☙☙The Pawtucket Falls are well known to the inhabitants of these Plantations.☙They are one of the wonders of the state.☙☙Many a good story has been told of the audacity of Sam Patch, the original American "bridge-jumper," and other hair-brained individuals, in throwing themselves from the mill or the bridge overlooking the Falls in the days of long-ago—but the charm of the present time is in watching the roaring and dashing of the waters which attract and fascinate the onlooker, especially in the early Spring when the Blackstone is rushing tumultuously to join the Seekonk.☙☙☙From the roadway on the bridge, looking "up-stream," the Slater Mill may be seen to the left, readily known by its little belfry.☙This was the birth-place of the cotton industry in the United States.☙☙☙"Down-stream," on the left, tower the mills of D. Goff & Sons, where "Goff's Braid" is manufactured.☙☙ Beyond the Falls, over the hills, a great number of the fine residences of Pawtucket will be found, and a ride over either the Central avenue, Lonsdale or Broadway electrics, which traverse the east side, will take you through the best home-section of the city.

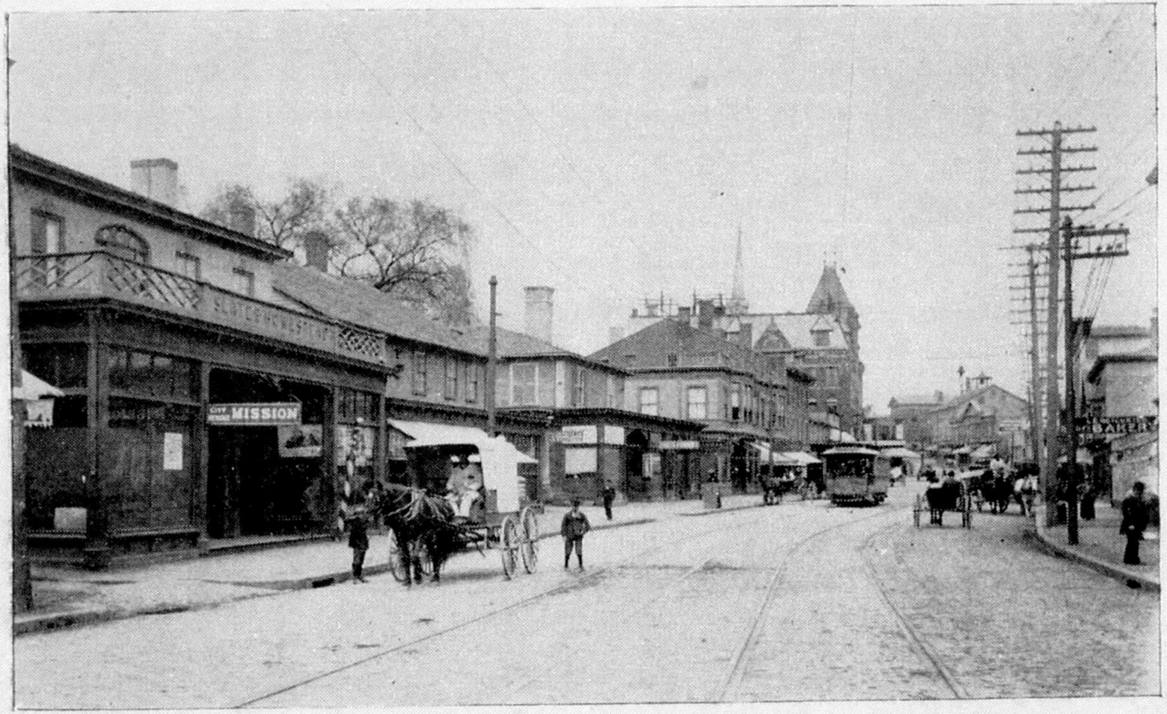

EAST AVENUE AND HIGH STREET, PAWTUCKET.

EAST AVENUE AND HIGH STREET.

❧ ❧ ❧

❧❧❧❧East avenue has recently been remodeled and widened.❧❧❧It has been improved in every respect, and makes an expansive business street to relieve the central portion of the city of a rather narrow and crowded aspect.❧❧❧Two lines of the electric service to Providence make their terminus at the junction of Main street and East avenue.❧❧ Opposte, at the corner of High and Main, the Interstate Line to Attleboro, North Attleboro, Plainville, Hebronville and Dodgeville, make connections.❧Taking one of the electrics at the Great Bridge, Providence, to Pawtucket, and transferring here for either of the places named—will give a very pleasant afternoon's outing at a slight cost—5 cents to Pawtucket, 10 cents on the Interstate—30 cents for the round trip, and through a fine country district.❧❧For another agreeable trip, take one of the cars from Providence, and transfer to the Lonsdale electrics, taking in Central and Valley Falls to Lonsdale, where the water scenery about is very pleasing, and a ride through the villages gives one a good idea of the homes of Rhode Isl^nd's factory workers.❧❧❧This trip will cost, all ways round—20 cents from Providence.❧❧

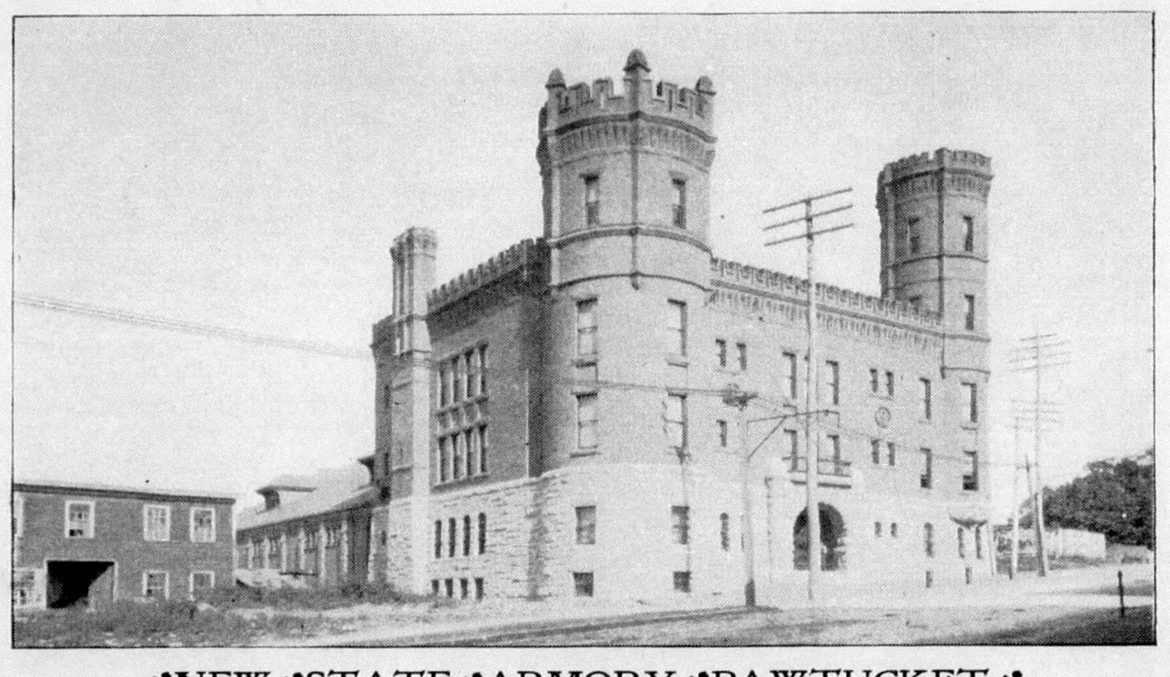

NEW STATE ARMORY PAWTUCKET

Exchange and Fountain Streets.

The King of Visible Writing Machines.

The "Williams"

Easiest machine in the world to operate
No. 1. Standard. Takes 8¾ in. paper

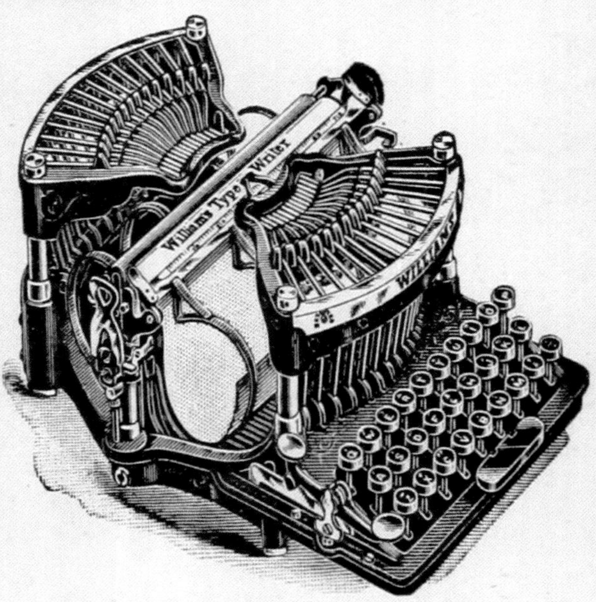

No. 3. Wide Carriage. Takes 14in. paper
Runs as easily as the smaller

ACTUAL VISIBLE WRITING

NO CARRIAGE TO LIFT

25% more work easily done on THE WILLIAMS than on any other machine ✤✤ Unlimited Speed Unquestionably the BEST for Expert or Novice

The American Book Exchange

Agents for Rhode Island

Francis Building 146 WESTMINSTER STREET

No trouble to show the Machine ✤ Purchasers Taught Typewriting without extra charge. ✤

THE ARMORY.

❧❧❧The New State Armory, corner of Exchange and Fountain streets, is one of the most notable of the new buildings in Pawtucket.❧It was completed in 1895, and was dedicated by a grand ball at which the distinguished military and civic officers of the state, with their ladies, appeared.❧❧The Armory is a splendidly equipped home for the military companies centering in Pawtucket, Troop A, Rhode Island Cavalry, Company G, Second Regiment Light Infantry, and Company H, First Regiment Infantry—and with a wise forrthought, space has been arranged for the accommodation of two more companies in the future.❧❧There is a grand drill room, a rifle-range and a bowling alley to be completed later, and separate rooms for each company's use, in all matters of detail the convenience of the soldier having been consulted to the nicest point.❧ The architects were Messrs. William R. Walker & Son, and the builders Messrs. Houlihan & Maguire, and both firms are entitled to the thanks of all good citizens for this fine structure.❧❧Cost bout $85,000. ❧It is open to the inspection of the public, and the Armorer, who is in attendance each week day, will take pleasure in showing his charge.❧❧The view which can be had from the tower is a fine one.

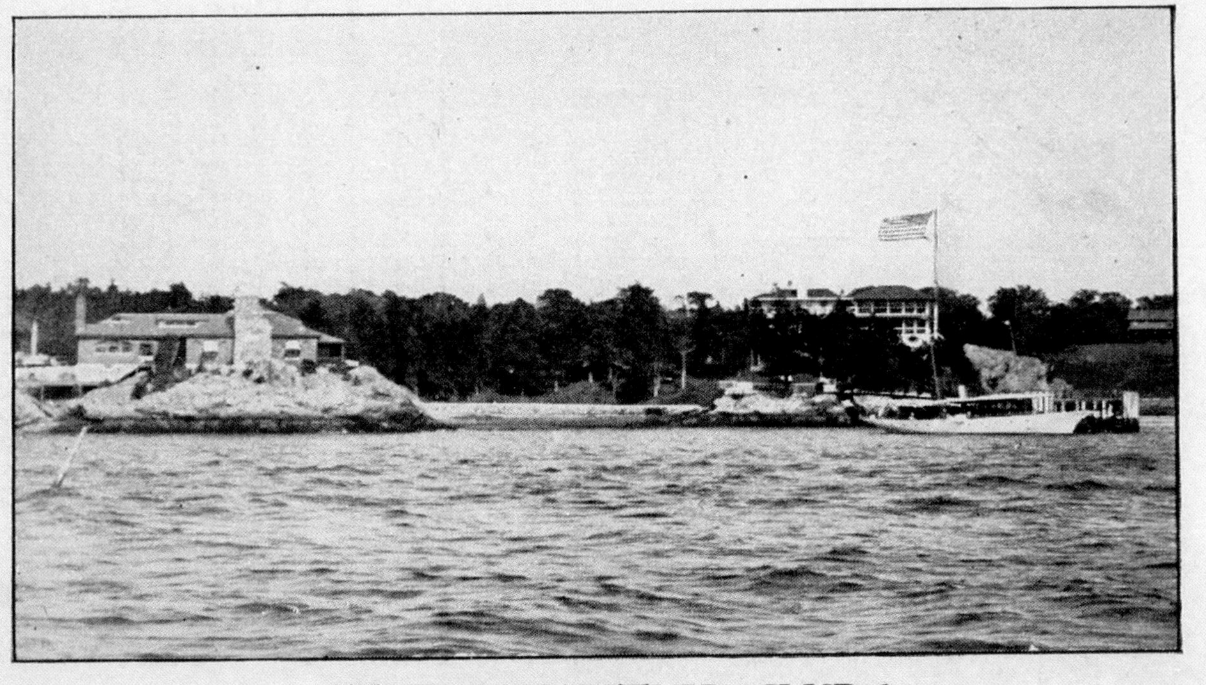

THE SQUANTUM CLUB
On the River Front

☙ SQUANTUM. ☙

☙☙☙

☙☙☙The Squantum Club, whose buildings occupy two prominent little rocky islets a short distance down the Bay, is located in East Providence.☙The Association is composed of a number of the leading men of Providence and Pawtucket, their principal aim and interest centering here in rest, recreation, and excellent dinners.☙☙☙Their repasts have become famous, and many of the distinguished men of the nation have been entertained here, Presidents Grant and Arthur among others.☙☙The grounds are not open to the public—a special invitation being necessary to obtain admittance.☙☙☙THE POMHAM CLUB, a younger association, with aims of a similar nature, has a fine club-house just below Silver Spring.☙It is located on a commanding position, giving a fine view of the river and the gay throng of steamers and sailing craft which pass continually in the bright summer days.☙☙FIELD'S POINT, the first resort of importance on the Bay, is on the west side, and is the most convenient of access☙☙☙A trip from the city, with time for the enjoyment of one of their excellent clam dinners can be made in two hours.☙☙☙Excursion tickets, round trip, 20 cents.☙☙Dinner, 50 cents.☙☙☙

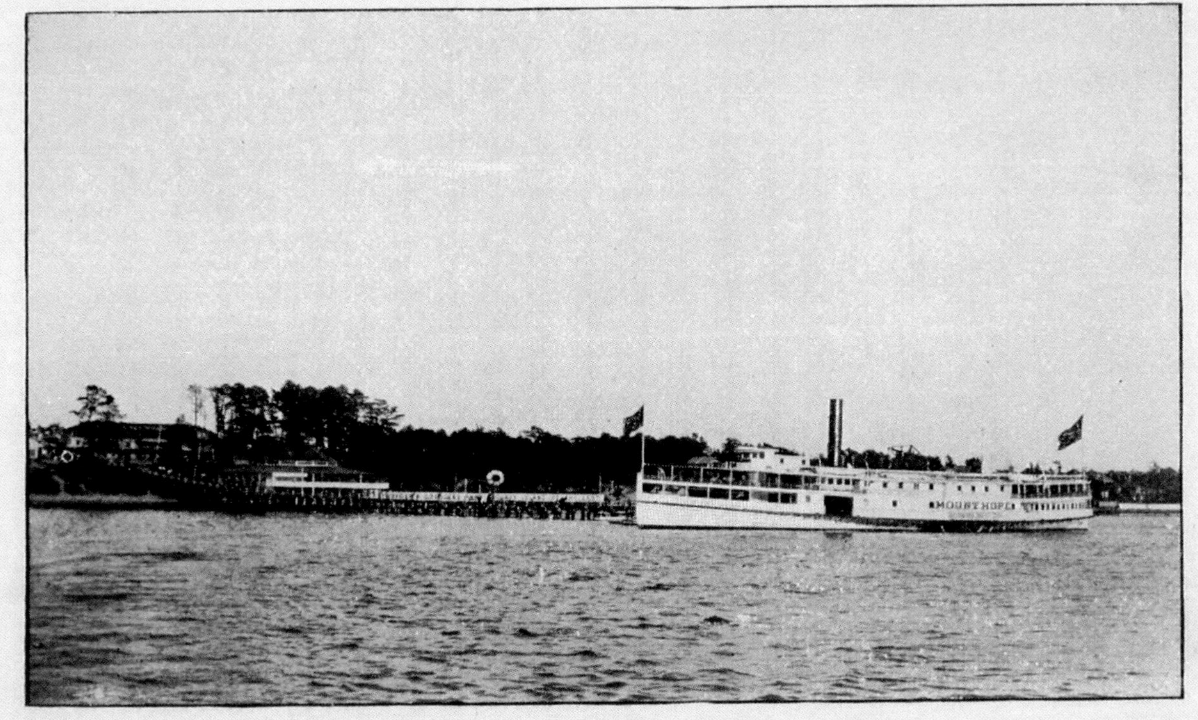

CRESCENT PARK LANDING.

CRESCENT PARK.

❧ ❧ ❧

❧❧❧Coney Island has its prototype to a certain extent in the well-known resort now called Crescent Park, a half-hour's sail from the city.❧This is the place for the crowd, having nearly all the popular amusements of the great New York resort, and furnishing music, dancing, bowling alleys, shooting galleries, merry-go-rounds, and good facilities for bathing.❧For the coming season the American Band (D. W. Reeves, leader,) will give the grand concerts which in other years have made Nantasket Beach the centre of interest as a shore place.❧A light opera will be one of the afternoon and evening attractions, the performances being given in a novel floating palace.❧It will be produced with great splendor by more than seventy leaders of the American opera companies, and at popular prices.❧❧❧A fine new cycle track is one of the prominent additions to the Park, and many of the famous bicycle champions will be seen here this season.❧❧The means of conveyance to the grounds are by the steamers, 20 cents for the round trip—steam cars, 17 cents each way—and by the electrics, 20 cents for the rounds. The clam dinners are first-class, at 50 cents.❧❧❧ The tea-rooms furnish refreshments of other kinds to those who do not care for a clam dinner.❧❧❧

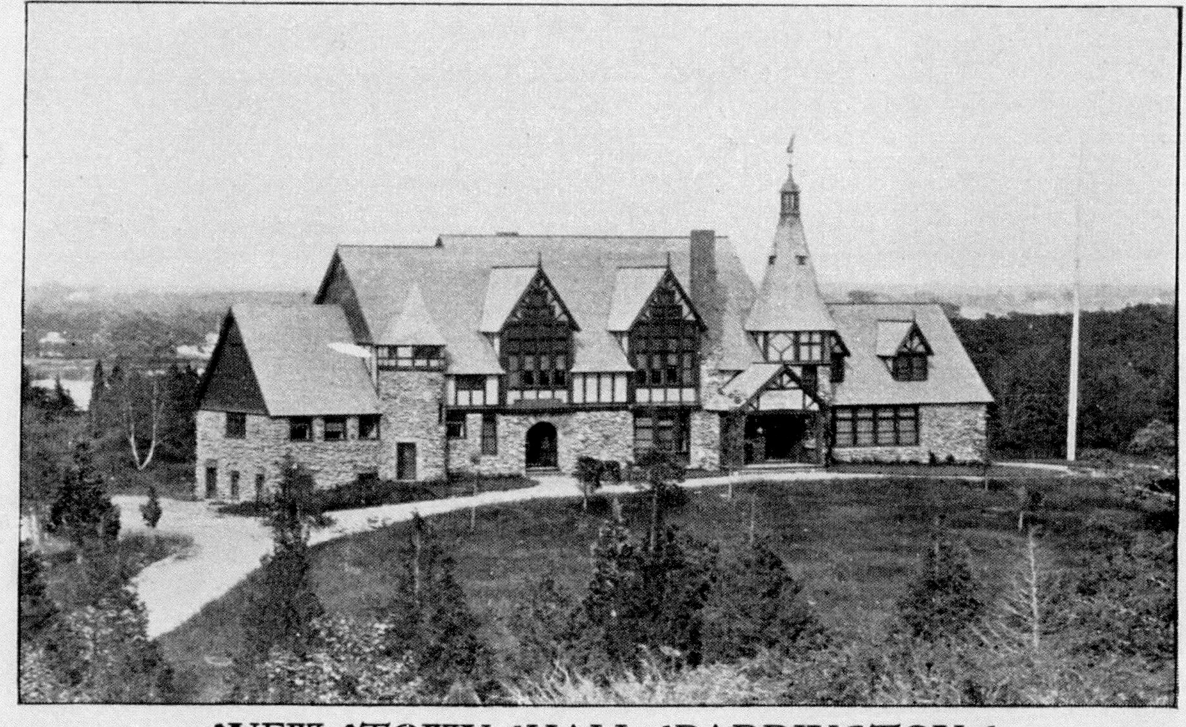

NEW TOWN HALL BARRINGTON

❧ BARRINGTON. ❧

❧ ❧ ❧

❧❧❧One of the most delightful residence towns within a reasonable train distance of Providence is Barrington.❧Within recent years many enterprising business men of Providence and Pawtucket have made their summer homes within its borders.❧ Through their assistance and public spirit the good roads of this town have, if possible, been made better still, and the drives all about are excellent.❧❧One can drive with great pleasure in any part of the town—Drownville, Nayatt Point and Barrington Centre are all good objective points.❧❧❧THE TOWN HALL, one of the most tasteful and best-located public buildings in the suburban towns of the State, is entitled to the affectionate admiration of the citizens whose enterprise made its erection possible.❧There are many fine residences in the town, especially on Rumstick and Nayatt Points.❧The fishing grounds off Nayatt Point are the favorite resorts for the east-side followers of Izaak Walton. ❧And next to these in their regard comes Kelley's Bridge, on the borders, next to the Town of Warren. ❧❧❧The river and bay views about Barrington are picturesque, and it is natural that it should increase in favor as a suburban residence section.

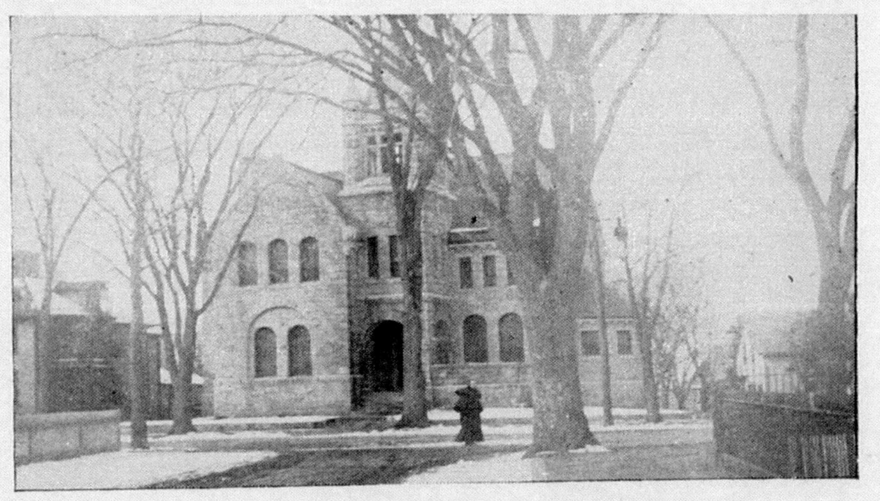

THE TOWN HALL, WARREN.

TOWN HALL, WARREN.

❧ ❧ ❧

❧❧The American coast is particularly favored in its bays and inlets, making charming localities for the planting of homes and communities along shore. ❧❧In one of these pleasant nooks lies the Town of Warren, east of the bay.❧❧❧Years ago it was one of the most prosperous of whaling ports, and much of the comfort of the present generation in that town is due to the skill, enterprise and pluck of the men who went "down to the sea in ships" before the war.❧❧❧Now it is a manufacturing town, with a large foundry, cotton mills and an extensive yarn and thread mill.❧❧❧The enterprise of the new Warren is illustrated in its neat and well-kept streets and sidewalks, and in the two notable buildings recently built on the main street, the Town Hall and the Public Library.❧❧These are institutions in which the citizens of Warren may well feel a just pride.❧❧❧The Warren Manufacturing Company, whose mills were destroyed by fire in the fall of 1895, is erecting a new manufactory with the most approved appliances and machinery, and will soon have one of the finest establishments in New England, giving the town a new impetus in a business way and a large addition to its population.❧❧❧❧

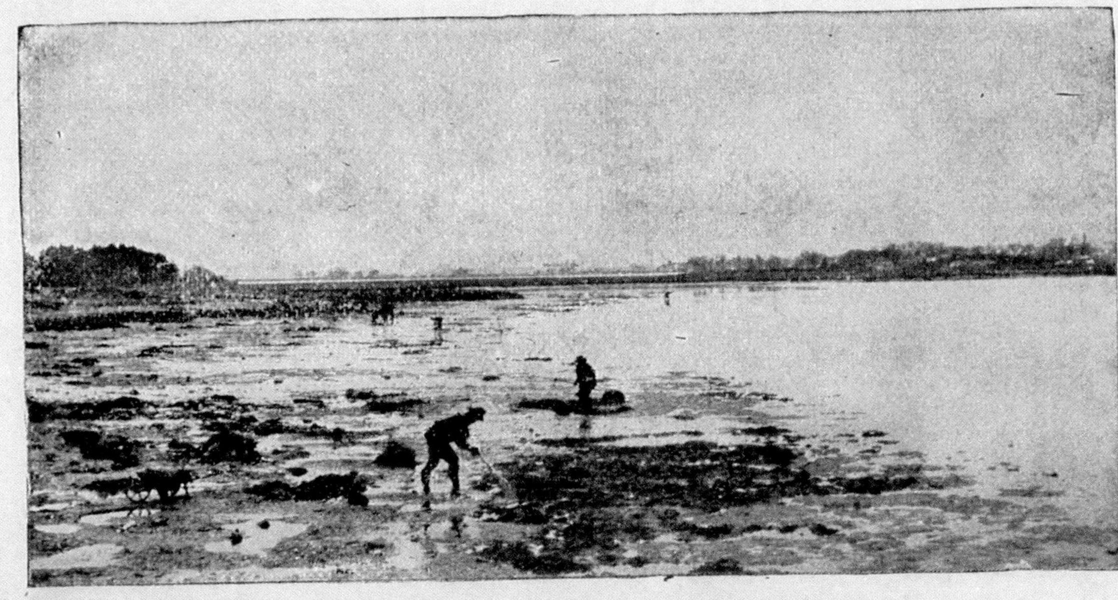

THE CLAM DIGGERS

Season of 1896.

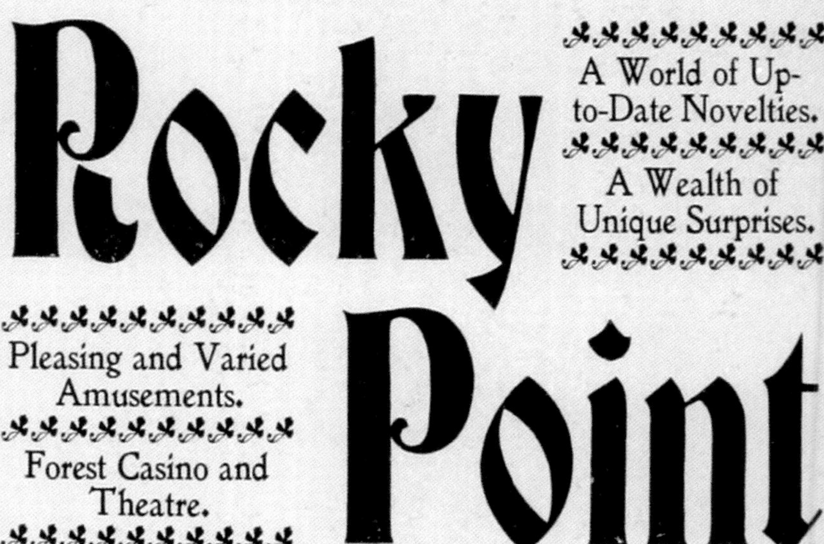

Nature's Seaside Garden.

2 – Big Vaudeville Shows—2. Seaview Garden and Concert Hall. "Shooting the Chutes," the Latest Fad. The Crystal Maze and X-Rays. Russian Toboggan, Merry-Go-Rounds and Swinging Boats, Bowling Alleys.

The Best Shore Dinner on the Bay.

Shooting Galleries, Dance Halls.
Vast Game Grounds, League Base Ball Games.

The Biggest, Best and Newest Attractions to be Found Anywhere.

R. A. HARRINGTON, Proprietor and Manager.

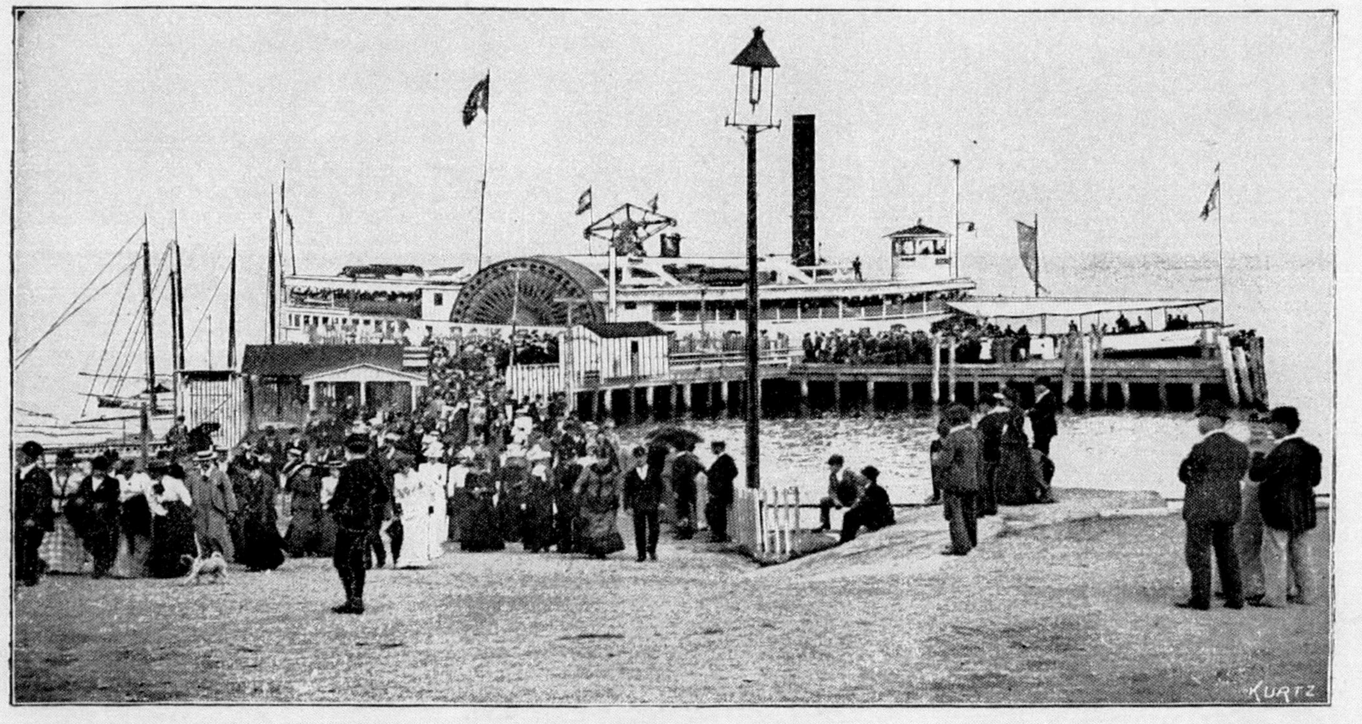

THE ROCKY POINT LANDING.

You Need Not

USE AN

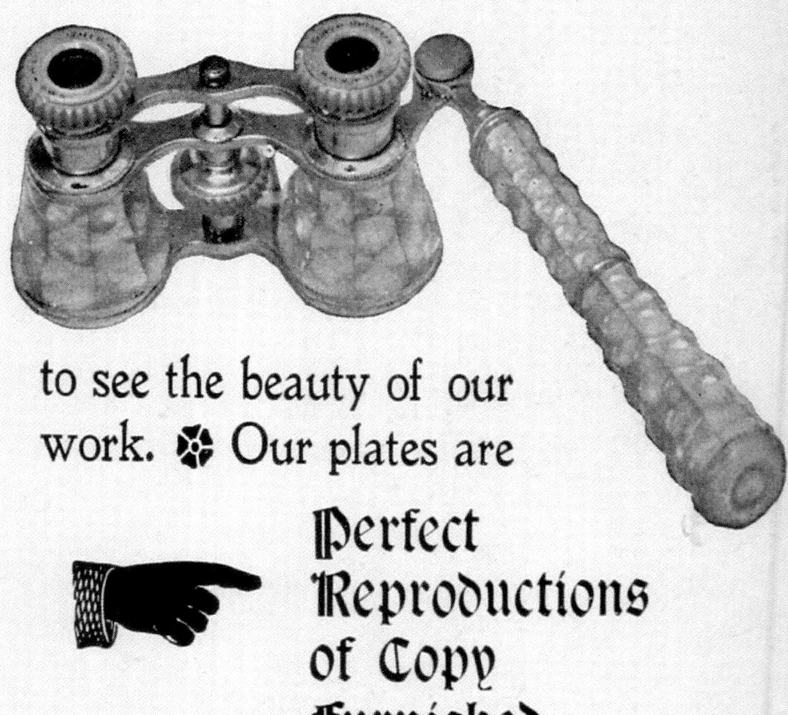

to see the beauty of our work. Our plates are

Perfect Reproductions of Copy Furnished

SEND FOR SAMPLES AND PRICES ON ANY KIND OF ENGRAVING

Franklin Engraving Co.

Makers of Superior Half-Tone and Relief Plates.

235 Washington Street, Boston, Mass.

The Plate of Opera Glass was Made Directly from Article.

ROCKY POINT.

☘ ☘ ☘

☘☘☘Most charming of all the beautiful spots so profusely scattered along the shores of world-famed Narragansett Bay, Rocky Point needs no addition to its natural attractions to captivate the visitor from abroad.☘☘The rock-bound shore of the extreme point softens gracefully on the north to the finest bit of sheltered bathing beach imaginable, while southward grassy slopes succeed the rocks that guard the point.☘☘Back from the commodious wharf where the steamers from Providence, Newport and Fall River land their passengers, the ground rises gently, the highest eminence being surmounted by a lofty observatory from which a fine view for miles around may be obtained. Scattered over the beautiful grounds, which cover many acres, are attractions almost without number.☘Toboggans, chutes, bowling alleys, swings, a Ferris wheel, etc., vie with each other in competition with the magnificent shore dining hall and the cosy theatre for the attention and amusement of the visitor.☘☘☘In the dining hall are served the shore dinners which have made Rocky Point famous the world over.☘In the theatre one may witness the best talent obtainable in dramatic, operatic and vaudeville performances.

☙ BRISTOL. ☙

☙ ☙ ☙

☙☙☙Like its parent in England, Bristol is a famous town.☙It has recently given the world a wonderful ship, the "Defender," and it has always had a wide reputation on the water.☙☙☙The "Yankee" privateer was a Bristol craft, and many a good sailor has been nurtured and sent forth from this old town. ☙☙The Bristol Naval Reserve have an enviable reputation among Uncle Sam's coast defenders to-day, and the State has recently put up for them a substantial home on the water front.☙☙☙The founders of the town were men of foresight, and in laying out the place made wide streets and regular squares, which have been continued and improved by their descendants.☙☙☙These streets are to-day beautfied and splendidly shaded by that glory of New England, the elm, making Bristol one of the finest of Rhode Island towns.☙☙The famous Herreshoff works, the great workshops of the National Rubber Company, the Cranston Woolen and the Naumkeag Cotton Mills are located here, keeping well in touch with the manufacturing centres of the rest of the state.☙☙The drives about the town are good, there are many fine summer residences being built, and it may yet be a second Newport.☙☙☙

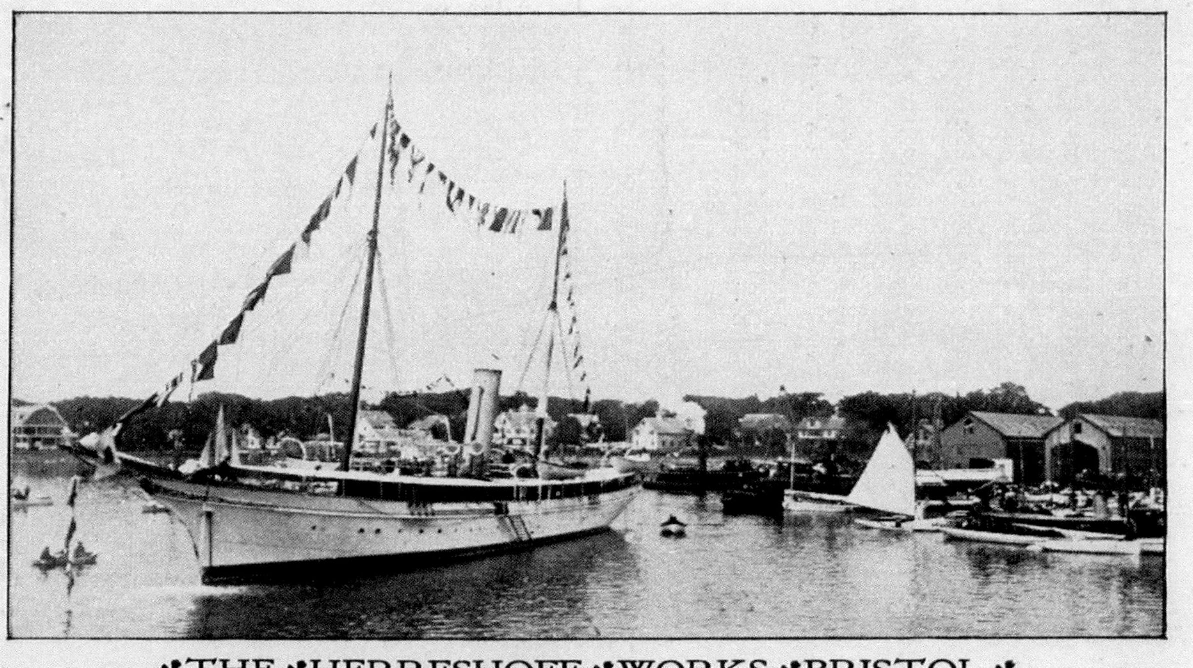

THE HERRESHOFF WORKS BRISTOL

Launch of the "Defender"

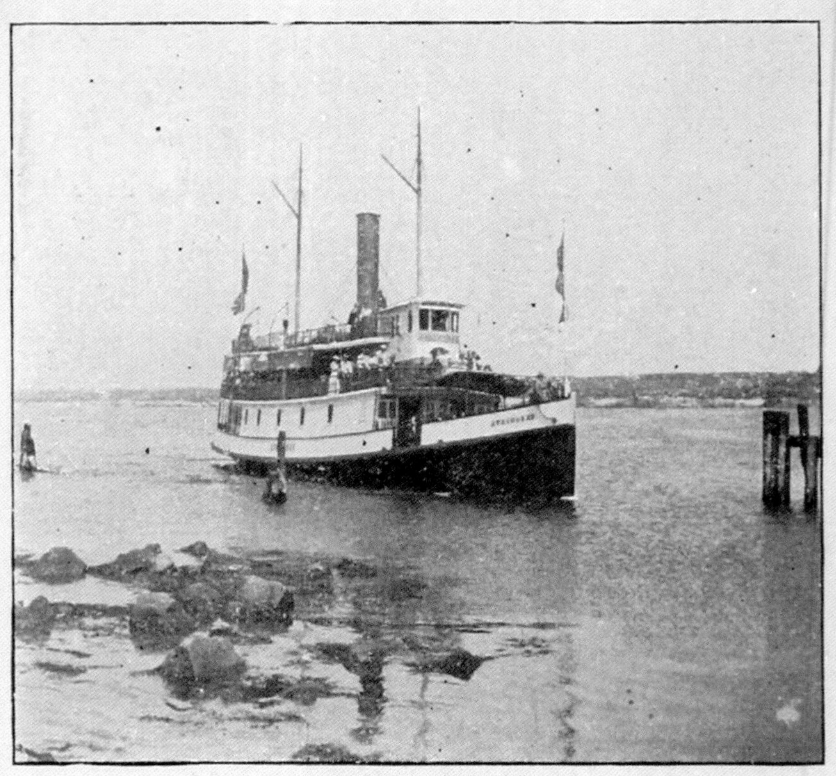

TO SEACONNET POINT.

An Ideal Excursion.

For the most delightful and enjoyable sail possible, take either of the roomy and comfortable steamers,

Awashonks and Queen City,

of the Seaconnet Steamboat Company, for

SEACONNET POINT.

One of the most charming bits of Rhode Island's shore. En route, the usual course of the bay steamers is taken until Pappoosesquaw Point is reached, then past Bristol Ferry, Stone Bridge and the entire length of Seaconnet River to the Point, where about three hours are given excursionists to enjoy the natural beauties of the place. The boats leave foot of Planet street, Providence, at 10 A. M. The fare for the round trip is $1.00; single tickets, 75 cents.

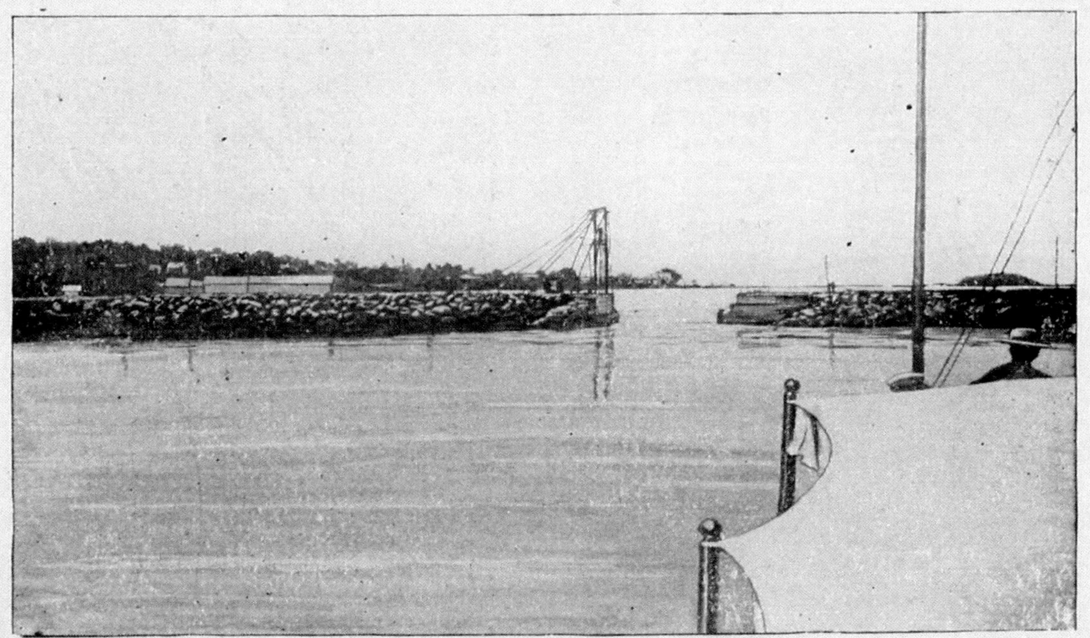

THE STONE BRIDGE.

Between Tiverton and the Island of Rhode Island.

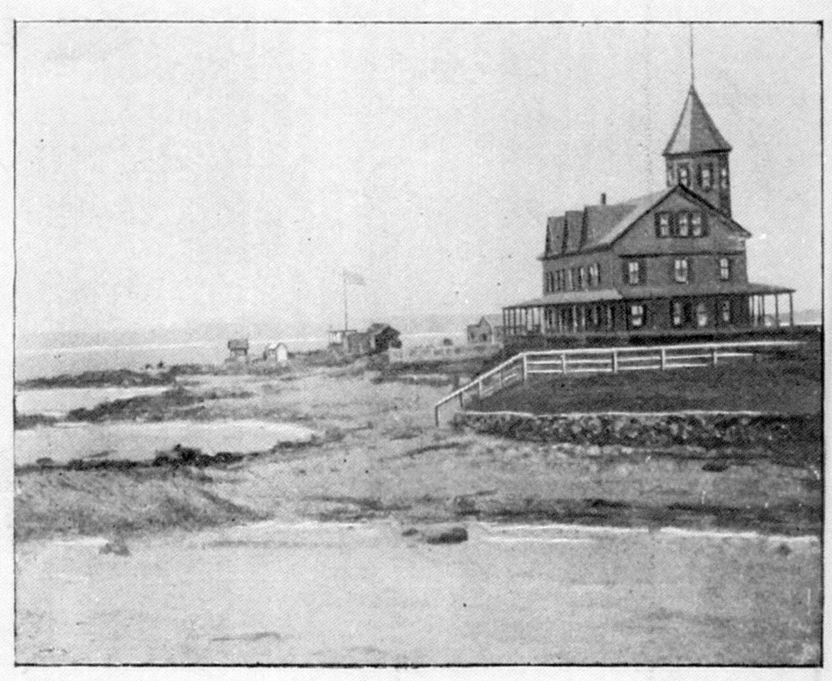

The
Sakonnet Hotel,

Sakonnet Point, R. I.

Now open for the Season of '96.
For Circular and particulars address

J. L. SLOCUM,

Telephone in the Hotel. Box 1034, Providence, R. I.

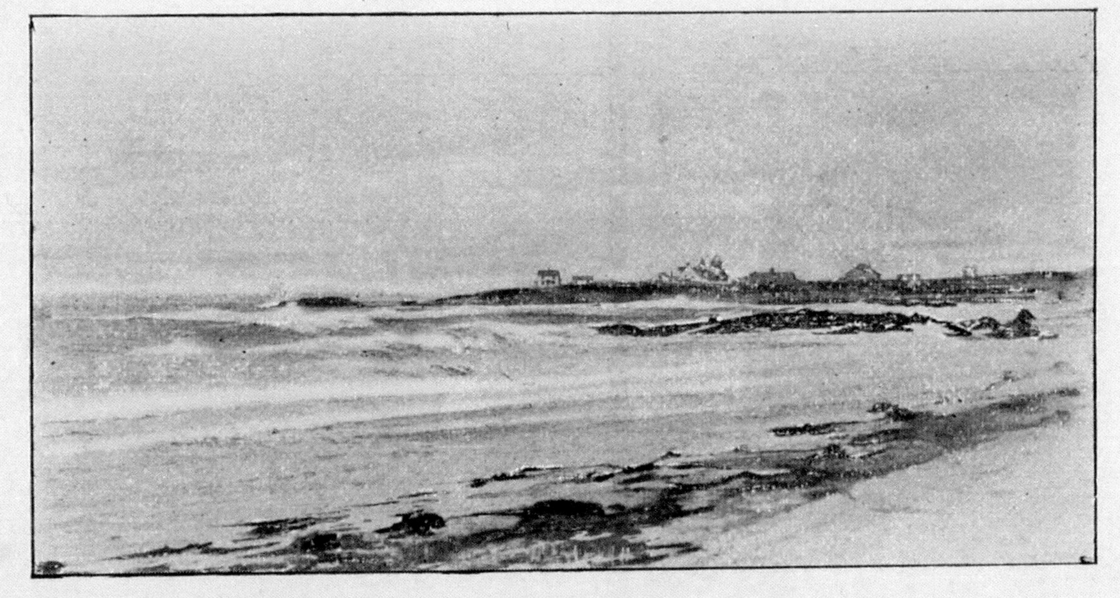

SEACONNET POINT AND THE BEACH.

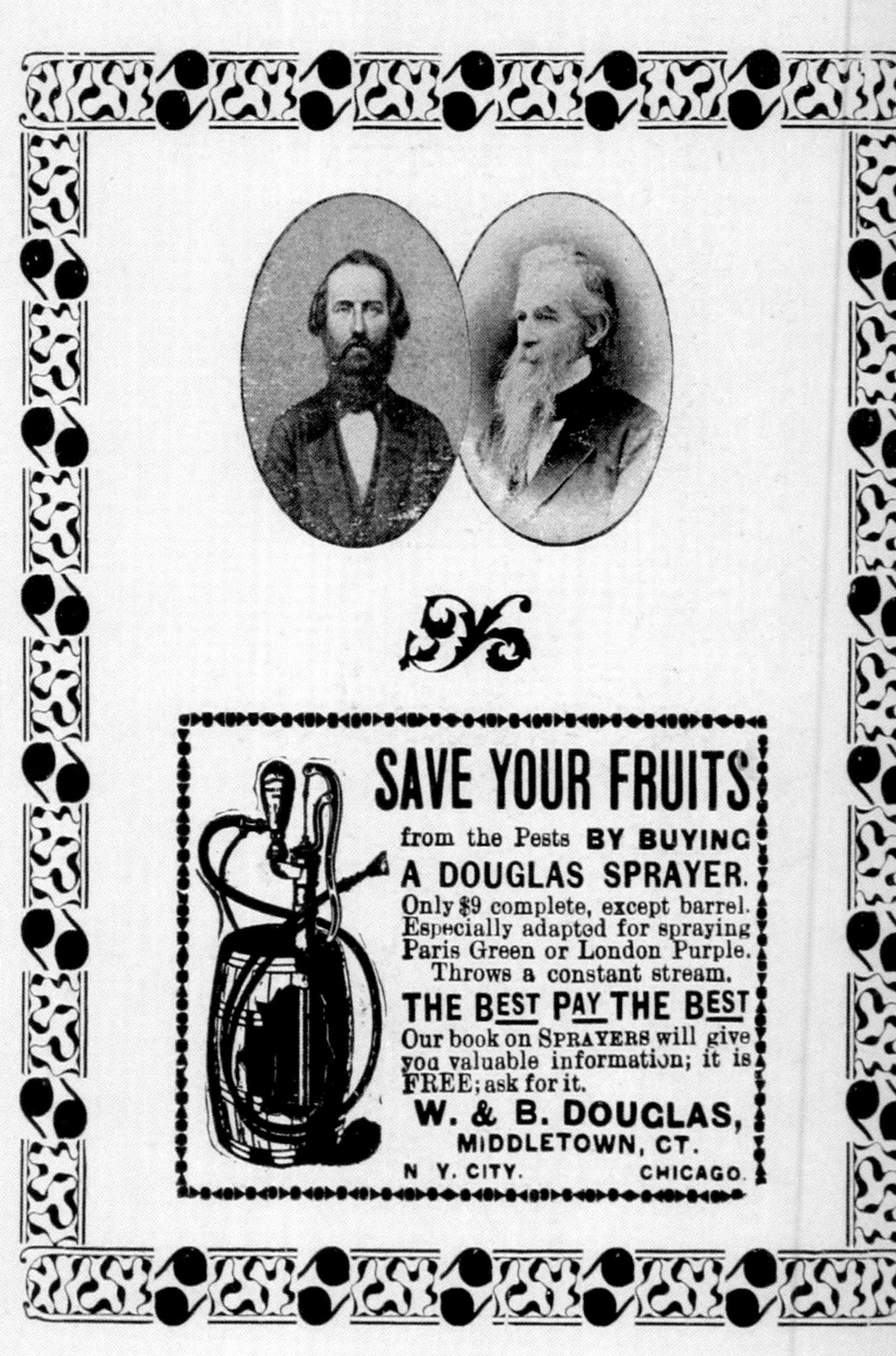
SAVE YOUR FRUITS
from the Pests BY BUYING
A DOUGLAS SPRAYER.
Only $9 complete, except barrel.
Especially adapted for spraying
Paris Green or London Purple.
Throws a constant stream.
THE BEST PAY THE BEST
Our book on SPRAYERS will give
you valuable information; it is
FREE; ask for it.
W. & B. DOUGLAS,
MIDDLETOWN, CT.
N. Y. CITY. CHICAGO.

SEACONNET POINT,

☙ ☙ ☙

☙☙In the Town of Little Compton, is situared on the southeastern extremity of the main-land of Rhode Island, at the mouth of the Seaconnet River, opposite Newport.☙It is noted for its varied scenery of rock-bound shores, its grand ocean views, its fishing and bathing.☙☙The steamers Awashonks and Queen City of the Seaconnet Boat Company make daily trips (Sundays included), leaving the wharf at foot of Planet street at 10 a. m., and returning from the Point at 3 p. m., giving the excursionist three hours at Seaconnet.☙☙☙Fare 75 cents for the round trip.☙☙From the city to Pappoosesquaw Point the course is about the same as that to Newport, but from here the scenery changes and we pass Hog Island, the Lightship, and into Bristol, giving a view of the Herreshoff boat shops. ☙Down by Bristol Ferry Light and the Ferry, we enter Mount Hope Bay, getting a view of Mount Hope and Fall River; then changing our course we pass Tiverton Heights, Church's Fish Works, through the railroad bridge, stopping at Tiverton Station Wharf; then through the narrow draw of Old Stone Bridge, out into Seaconnet River, stopping at White's Wharf, and then rounding into view of the ocean, arriving at the Point in time for dinner.

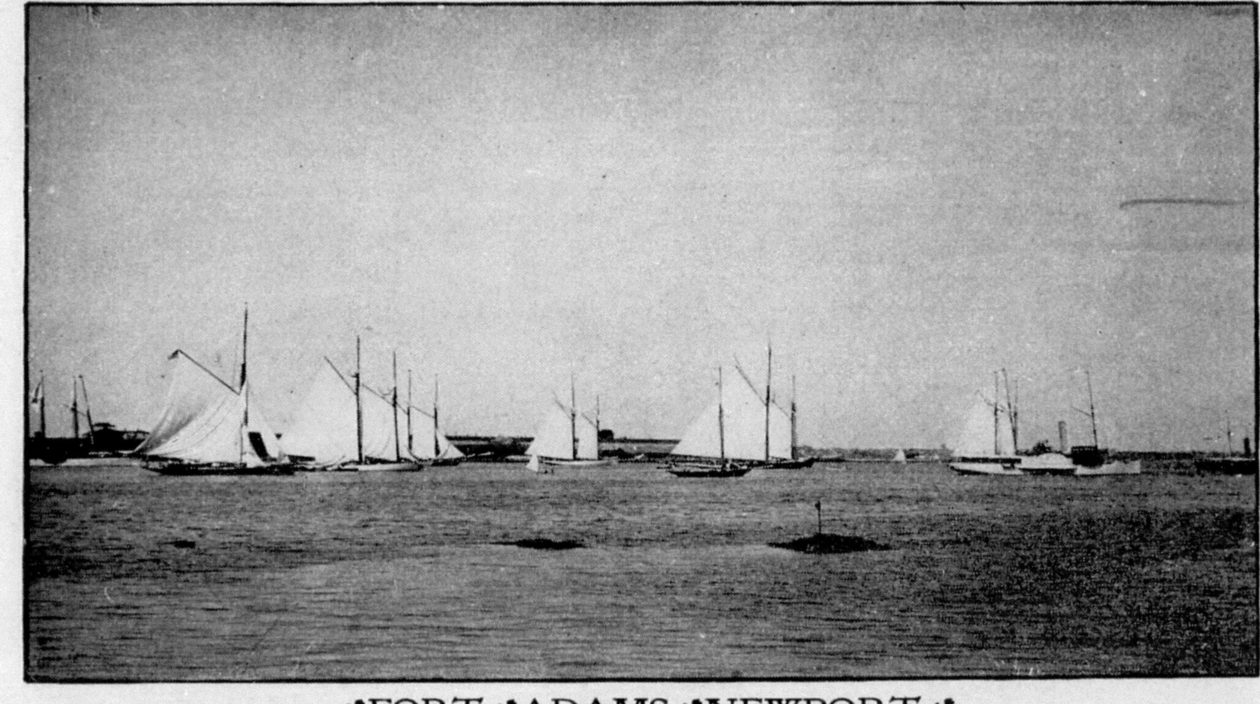

FORT ADAMS NEWPORT

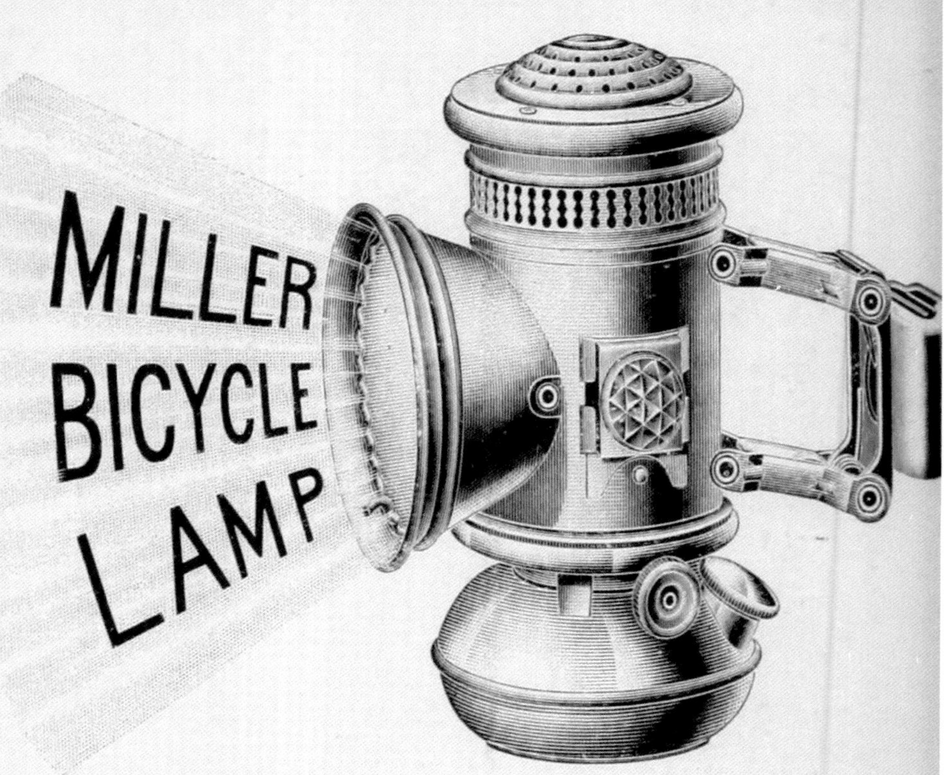

Latest and Best. Patents Applied For.

With 2½ Inch Double Convex Lens. Height, 5¾ Inches. Weight, 14 Ounces.

FULL NICKEL FINISH.

CLAIMS:

Absolutely the Best. Flame cannot be blown or jarred out. No other lamp can equal it in this respect.

Owing to special construction the oil cannot escape, and it will not sweat. It has a double convex, 2½ inch lens, projecting a most powerful and intense light. Both reflector at the back, and the funnel containing the lenses are protected from smoke by a combination of detachable lenses allowing all parts to be easily cleaned. The wick is held at any desired height by our end bearing drag attachment. No other lamp has this feature.

Made in U. S. A. by EDWARD MILLER & CO.

Manufacturers of the Celebrated "**Miller**," "**Juno**" and "**Rochester**" Lamps.

❧ NEWPORT. ❧

❧ ❧ ❧

❧❧Renowned in all civilized lands, this beautiful old city holds proud distinction over all other American outing spots.❧❧❧Attractions for a day, week, month, season or all the year round can be found to lure the visitor to remain within its borders.❧Its breezes in summer are invigorating and refreshing, and in winter balmy and health-giving. ❧On one's first approach by steamboat, the harbor in the summer time makes a picture to be remembered.❧❧❧The white-winged craft with which its waters are usually sprinkled; the Lime Rock Light, made famous by Ida Lewis; the elegant residences, with their bright green lawns, to the south; the dark gray walls of Fort Adams looming cautiously up in the distance; the Torpedo Station, to the right; and the city with its long wharves and quaint old storehouses, to the left, impress one with the fancy that it is the entrance to a fairy-land.❧❧ The older section of Newport, which first presents itself to the stranger upon getting beyond the landing, is apt to be a trifle disappointing, as the main business streets are narrow, as in many American seaport towns, and most of the buildings low and old-style in architecture.❧❧But the modern Newport,

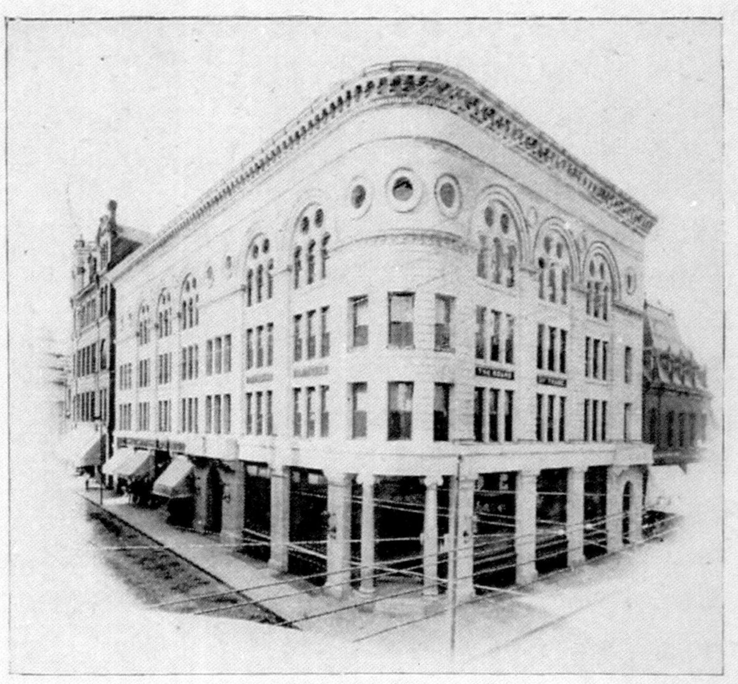

The
Merchants National Bank
Of New Bedford.

COR. PURCHASE AND WILLIAMS STREETS.

CAPITAL, $1,000,000
SURPLUS, $600,000

Capital and Surplus larger than any National Bank in Massachusetts, outside of Boston. Depositors offered every facility which their balances, business and responsibility warrant. Correspondence invited.

GILBERT ALLEN,
President.

H. C. W. MOSHER,
Cashier.

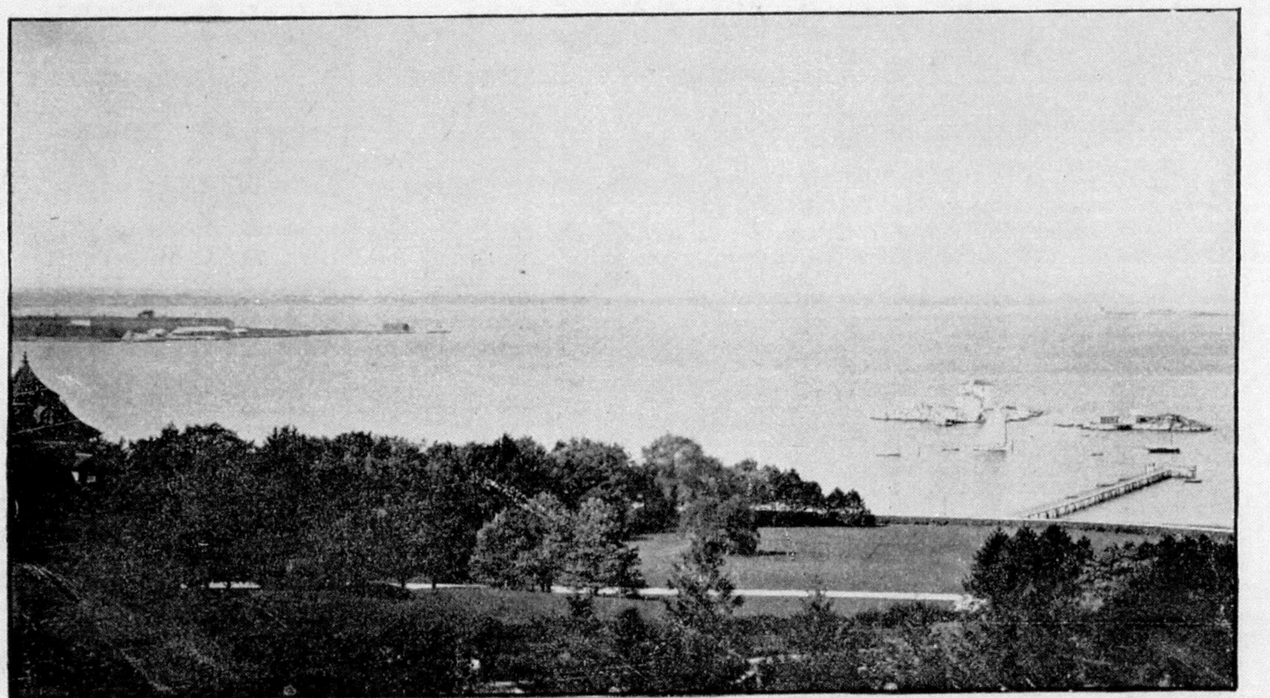

LIME ROCK LIGHT AND FORT ADAMS

❧ ❧ ❧

which is the chief centre of attraction to all visitors, lies mainly in other directions, and sustains fully the promise of the first picture.❧❧To get the greatest amount of pleasure from a day's stay in Newport one should take an electric after getting ashore and go first to the Beach, where an hour can be passed in watching the rolling of the surf and the frolics of the bathers, and in strolling on the sands.❧Dinner can be had in the halls near by, and then the CLIFFS can be taken in as far as THE FORTY STEPS in a walk which will give a glorious view of the Atlantic.❧❧❧If inclined for a long walk, continue along the Cliffs for three miles or so and note the beautiful cottages which give the reputation that has brought to the city the wealthiest men in the country in search of summer homes.❧This is the most delightful walk on the coast and will place in the memory a picture which will linger for all time.❧❧❧If not disposed for so long a walk, at the Forty Steps take Narragansett avenue, passing many elegant villas, to Bellevue avenue; then take a "barge" down this celebrated boulevard, get near to the driver and have him point out to you Senator Wetmore's house, the "Marble Palace," the

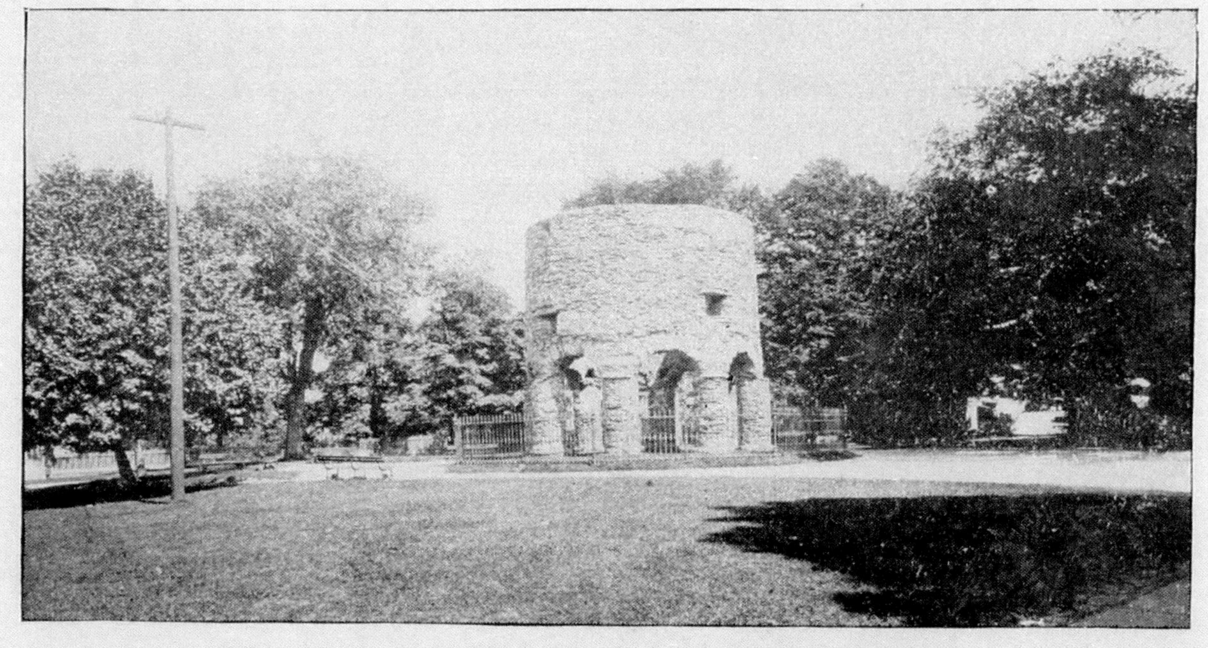

THE OLD STONE MILL, NEWPORT.

Touro Park.

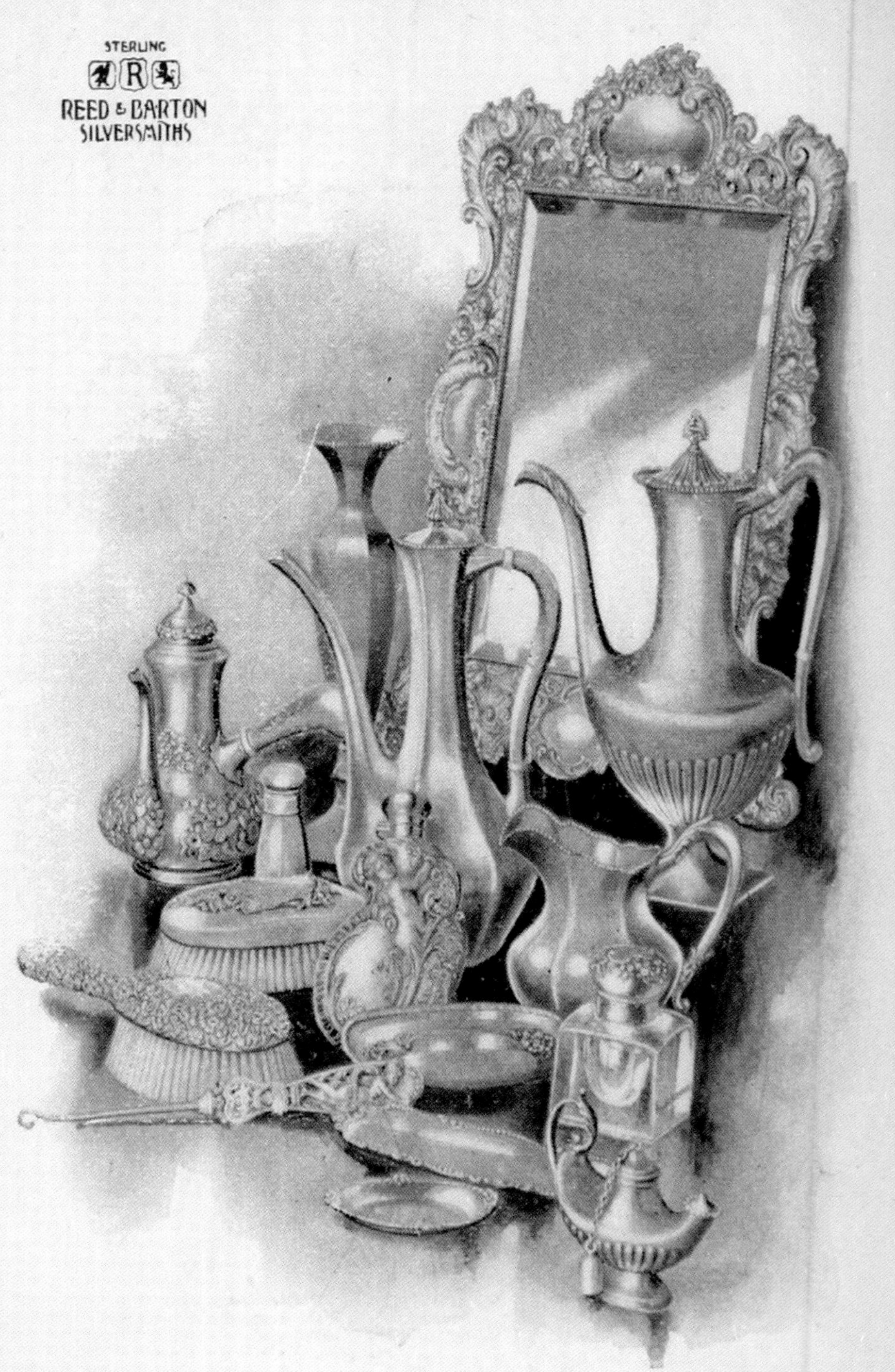

Reed & Barton, SILVERSMITHS,

Factory and Offices, Taunton, Mass.

Salesrooms,
41 Union Square and
13 Maiden Lane, N. Y.

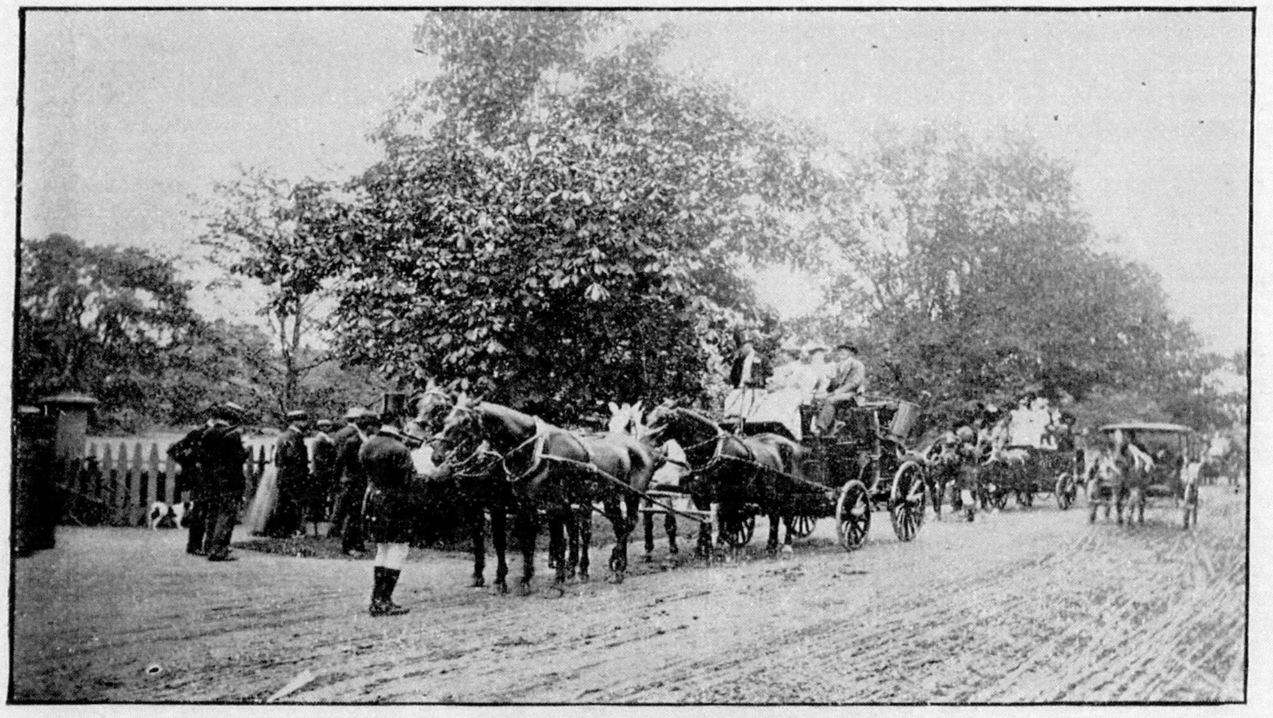

A FOUR-IN-HAND DRIVE

Bellevue Avenue, Newport

✤ ✤ ✤

Belmont and Astor cottages, the latest, Cornelius Vanderbilt's unpretentious home, and stop at Bailey's Beach, enjoy the breakers here for a few moments, cross the smooth white sands to the rocks beyond, creep over the hill, visit the Spouting Rocks, hear the roar of the waters as they dash in and out, watch the fishermen and spend what time can be spared in lolling about, breathing in the bracing air, and leave it regretting that you cannot spend many hours more here. ✤✤ PIC-NIC parties make these rocks their dining hall, and a better spot for an out-door banquet it would be difficult to select. ✤✤ The return to the city can be made by the same kind of conveyance. ✤✤✤ It will take the passenger by the Ocean House, a hotel with a fame nearly as great and as old as that of the city; past the Casino to the dainty little Touro Park, where may be seen The Old Stone Mill, still an object of wonder and mystery; and the statue to Commodore Matthew C. Perry, who negotiated the first treaty with Japan in 1854. ✤✤ Opposite the Park, to the south, the Channing Memorial Church attracts the attention of the visitor by its notable architecture. ✤ Along Bellevue the Redwood Library is seen, and still further

MR. A. O'D. TAYLOR,

Real Estate Agent, ☙ ☙ 124 Bellevue Avenue, Newport, R. I.,

☙☙☙Continues to place his services at the disposal of those ladies and gentlemen who may desire to learn prices for renting summer villas, generally known as "cottages," of which some simple specimens may be seen along the Cliffs and on Bellevue avenue.☙☙He also offers estates for sale, near the Cliffs, over Rocky Farm and the southern or fashionable part of the island; also building sites in and around the city; also farms of all sizes in the townships of Middletown and Portsmouth; houses for private residence in the "Hill" district and elsewhere at present procurable at unusually moderate prices.☙☙☙Residence all the year round in Newport and identification with its interests enable Mr. Taylor and his sons, who are associated with him in business, to give continuous attention to the collection of rents and care of various estates entrusted to him.☙For investors he places money on 1st mortgage of real estate in and about Newport at 5 and 6 per cent., but declines dealing in any other securities.☙He also acts as Trustee and Administrator on Estates, and his valuations of real estate are recognized in the courts of law.☙Mr. Taylor takes acknowledgments of deeds as Notary Public for the State of Rhode Island, and as Commissioner of Deeds for Massachusetts, New York, New Jersey, Pennsylvania, Michigan, Wisconsin, Illinois and District of Columbia.☙☙☙Office hours, 9 a. m. till 6 p. m.☙☙Please address any letter of inquiry to "A. O'D. TAYLOR, NEWPORT, R. I."

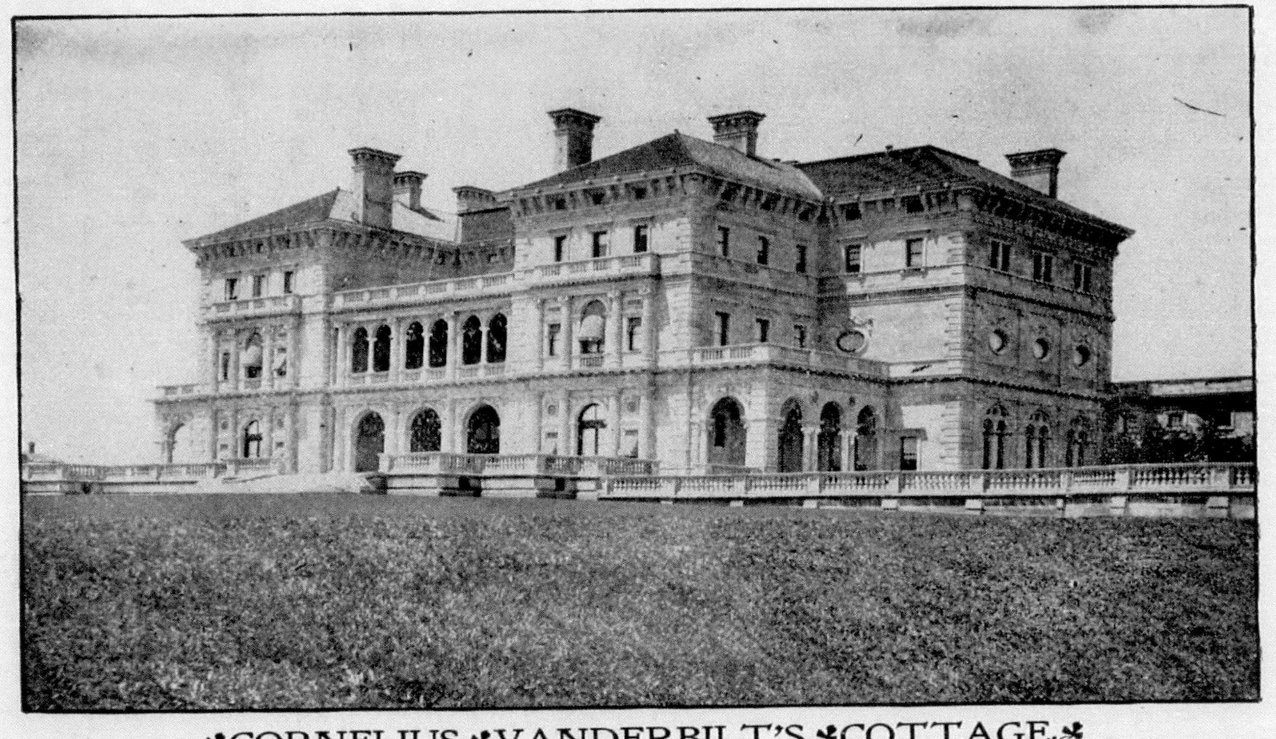

CORNELIUS VANDERBILT'S COTTAGE

Newport

Richmond Heaters.

STEAM AND HOT WATER.

Heating of Houses a Specialty.

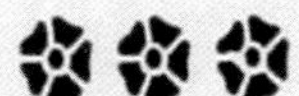

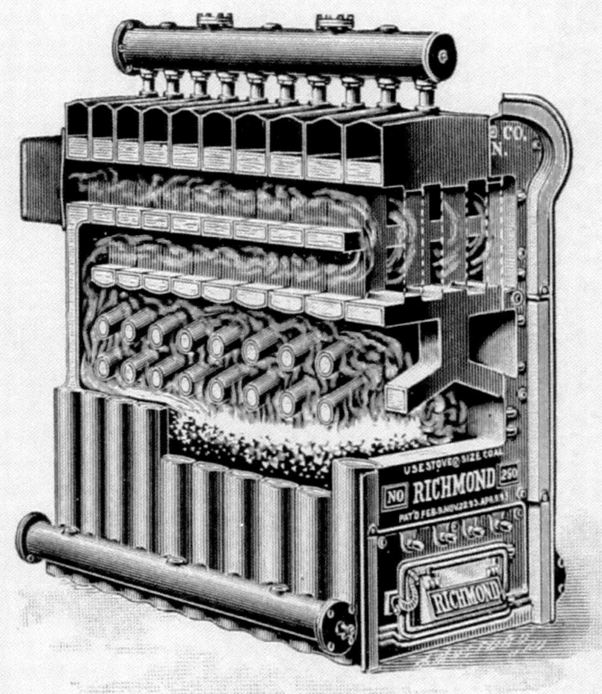

MANUFACTURED BY

THE RICHMOND STOVE CO., - NORWICH, CT.

RHODE ISLAND AGENCIES: H. T. Root & Son, Providence; Collyer Machine Co., Pawtucket; Barker Bros. & Co., Newport; J. F. Mulvey, Woonsocket; Fall River Steam and Gas Pipe Co. Corp., Fall River.

❧ ❧ ❧

along, on Touro street, the Jewish Synagogue.❧❧ The State House and the statue to Commodore Oliver Hazard Perry, the hero of Lake Erie, will be noticed by going through Touro street to the Parade and Mall.❧A good day's work has been done and much pleasure derived.❧❧The programme can be varied by a sail to Fort Adams or across to Jamestown which is becoming a hotel centre, a visit to Old Trinity Church, or a trip to PURGATORY, beyond Easton's Beach.❧❧The cost of the whole trip is light.❧❧❧The ten-mile drive which takes in pretty much all that is worth seeing can be made at a reasonable price if you make a careful bargain with the coachman in wating at the dock. For hotel accommodations, THE AQUIDNECK, THE PERRY and OCEAN HOUSES can be recommended.❧There are many notable turnouts seen on the Newport roads, the Four-in-Hand parties are numerous, and the scene on the avenue about 5 o'clock, the fashionable time for driving, is animated and decidedly interesting.❧❧Taking the steamer of the Providence and Newport Line at 9 a. m., stopping in Newport and getting home by the Wickford Line at 7.40 gives a good opportunity to pass a grand day's outing without too much hurry.

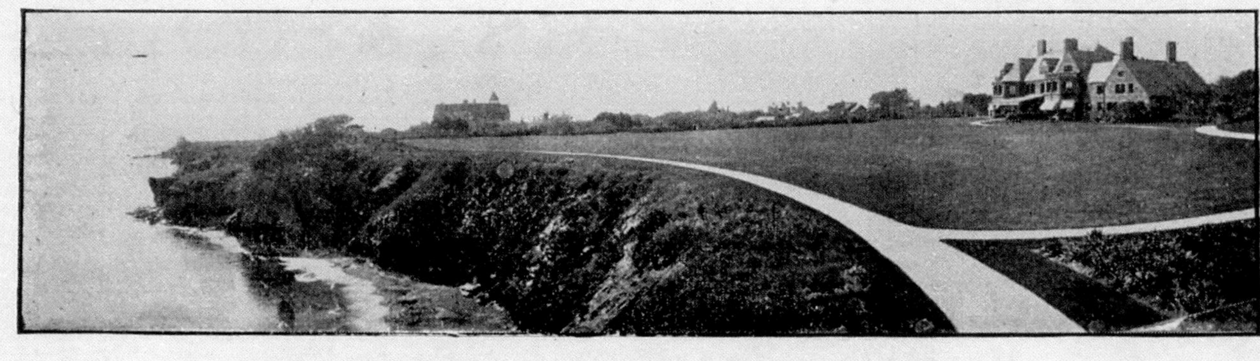

THE CLIFF WALK NEWPORT

NEWPORT & WICKFORD R. R. & STEAMBOAT CO.

THE WICKFORD ROUTE.

In effect June 15, 1896. Subject to change without notice.

From Newport.

TRAIN NOS.	1*	3*	5*	7*	9*	13*	15*	17*	19†
LEAVE	A M	A M	A M	P M	P M	P M	P M	P M	P M
NEWPORT Com'r'c'l Whf.	....	7 10	10 09	.....	1 20	.	4 20	‡7 40	11 15
WICKFORD JUNCT. *Arr.*	5 42	8 20	11 10	1 10	2 30	4 55	5 30	8 50	12 25
WICKFORD JUNCT...Lv.	5 43	8 23	11 22	.....	2 49	5 03	5 42	9 24	5 02
Providence..Union Depot "	6 35	8 55	11 57	....	3 24	5 55	6 15	9 54	A M 5 35
Boston ......Park Sq. Sta. "	8 45	10 15	1 15	. .	4 30	6 57	7 25	11 00	6 55
Wickford Junction.. Leave	....	8 32	11 40	2 09	2 40	4 58	6 35	8 52	1 55
Kingston ....Arrive	.. .	8 44	11 55	2 28	2 54	5 15	6 45	.. .	A M ....
Westerly.............. "	....	9 12	12 22	3 01	3 19	5 49	7 10	....	2 37
Stonington............ "	....	9 21	12 31	3 12	3 29	.....	.....	....	....
New London........... "	....	9 50	12 58	3 40	3 55	6 40	7 40	10 08	3 12
Saybrook.............. "	....	10 40	1 36	....	4 36	.....	.....	.....	....
New Haven............ "	....	11 52	2 25	....	5 25	9 05	9 05	11 37	4 45
Bridgeport... ... . "	....	12 29	2 57	....	5 56	9 36	9 36	12 25	5 18
New York... 42d St. Depot	....	2 00	4 30	....	7 30	11 00	11 00	B	7 00
Arrive	A M	P M	P M	P M	P M	P M	P M	A M	A M

To Newport.

TRAIN NOS.	2‡	4*	6*	8*	10*	14*	18*	16*	20*
LEAVE	Mid	A M	A M	A M	A M	P M	P M	P M	P M
New York....42d St. Depot	§12 03	...	5 00	.....	10 03	.....	1 02	.....	5 00
Bridgeport....................	1 33	...	7 05	.....	11 26	.. ..	2 25	...	6 20
New Haven....................	2 10	...	7 40	.....	12 05	.....	3 00	...	6 55
Saybrook	....	...	9 02	.....	12 58	.....	3 48	.....	7 41
New London..................	3 49	7 00	10 05	.....	1 34	3 30	4 27	.....	8 20
Stonington	....	7 33	10 30	.....	.....	4 00	4 52	.....	....
Westerly......................	4 24	7 43	10 39	.....	2 07	4 12	5 01	.....	8 50
Kingston	....	8 10	11 09	.....	2 35	4 49	5 29	.....	.....
Wickford Junction......Ar.	5 02	8 23	11 22	....	2 49	5 03	5 42	.....	9 24
Boston, Park Sq. Sta. Leave	12 03	6 45	10 03	10 25	P M 1 03	3 00	.....	3 45	7 00
Providence. ..Union Depot	A M 1 23	8 03	11 09	P M 1 20	2 09	4 15	.....	5 00	8 20
Wickford Junction......Ar.	1 55	8 32	11 40	2 09	2 40	4 58	.....	5 52	8 52
Wickford Junc..... Leave	5 15	8 32	11 40	2 10	2 49	5 03	5 44	5 52	9 24
Newport Com'r'c'l Whf.	6 30	9 45	1 00	.....	4 00	....	7 00	7 00	10 35
Arrive	A M	A M	P M	P M	P M	P M	P M	P M	P M

*Except Sundays. †Daily.

‡Through train between Wickford Junction, Philadelphia, Baltimore and Washington.

B Due Harlem River Station, New York, 2.05 a. m.; Philadelphia, 6.40 a. m.; Baltimore, 9.37 a. m.; Washington, 10.42 a. m.

§Following this train is the through Federal Express (via Harlem River) leaving Washington, 3.15 p.m.; Baltimore, 4.20 p.m.; Philadelphia, 6.50 p. m.; due at Wickford Junc., 5.14 a.m.; Newport, 6.30 a.m.

C. U. COFFIN, Agent, Newport, R. I.

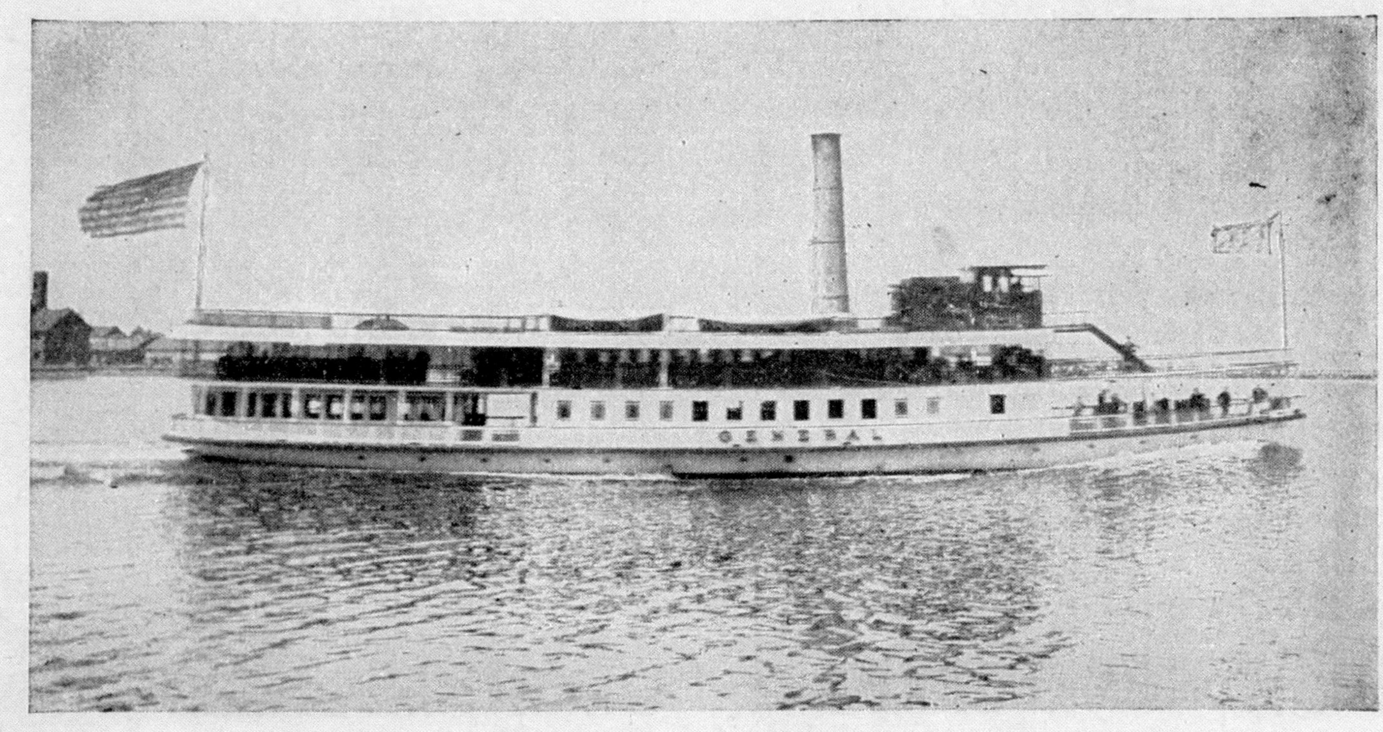

The Steamer "General" of the Newport & Wickford Line.

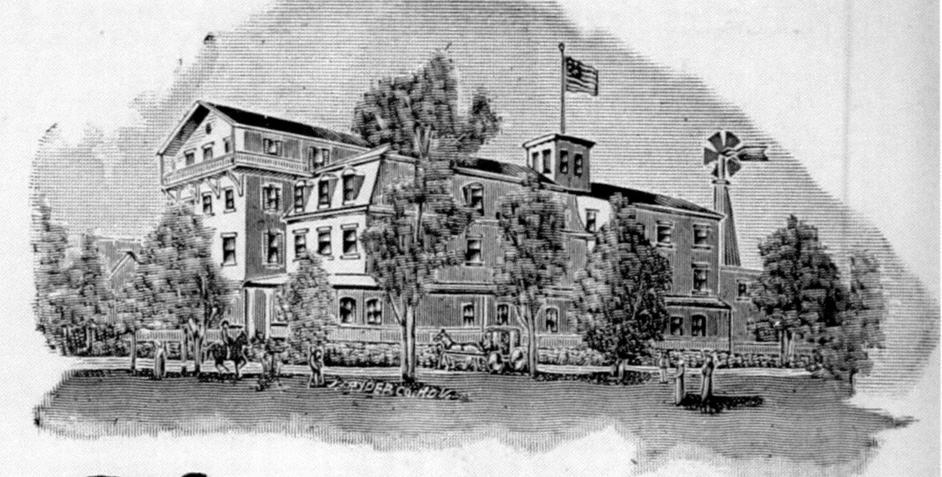

The Arlington

NARRAGANSETT PIER R.I.

DOGS NOT TAKEN.

Earnest L. Caswell.

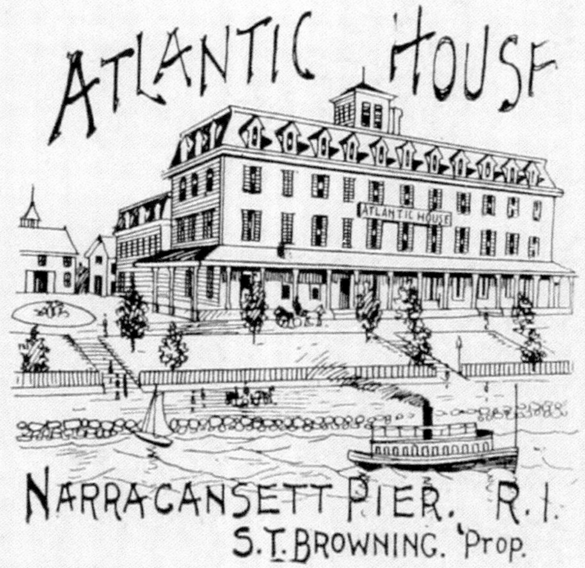

The most delightfully situated hotel at the Pier. Directly facing Ocean avenue and the ocean itself; about midway between the railroad station and the bathing beach, and but a minute's walk from the Casino.

The Atlantic is known as one of the most comfortable and popular houses on the New England coast.

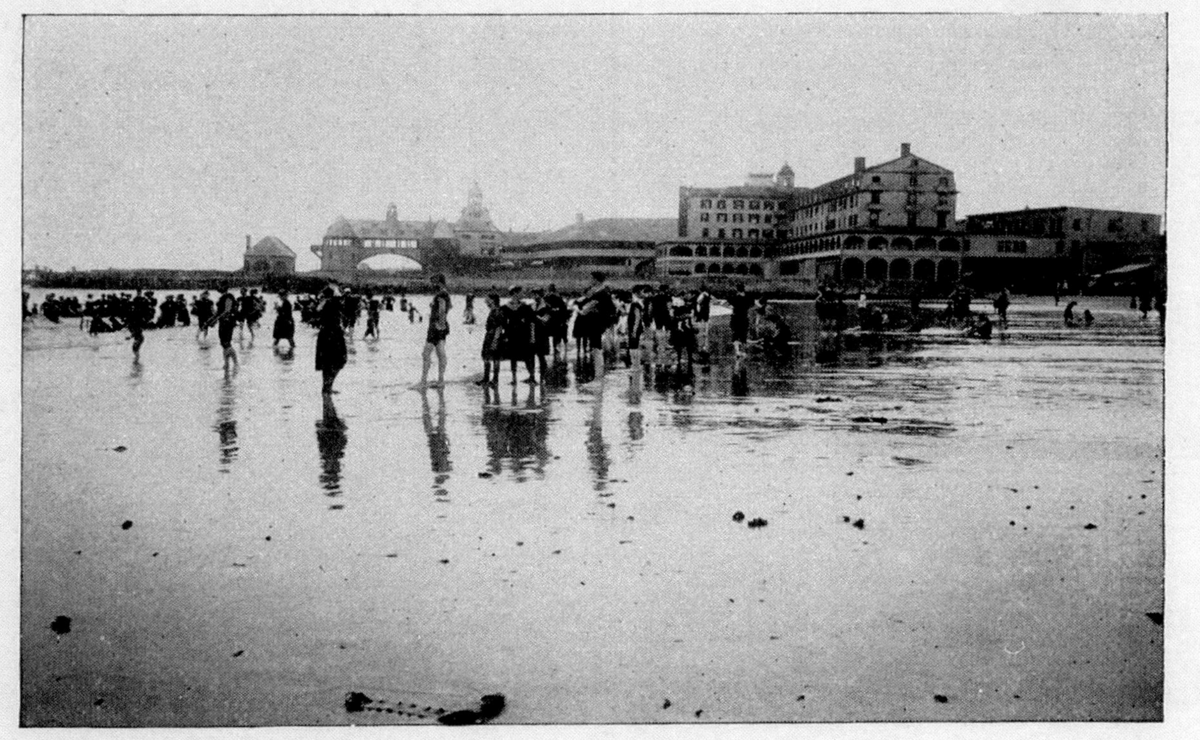

THE BEACH AND CASINO,

Narragansett Pier, R. I.

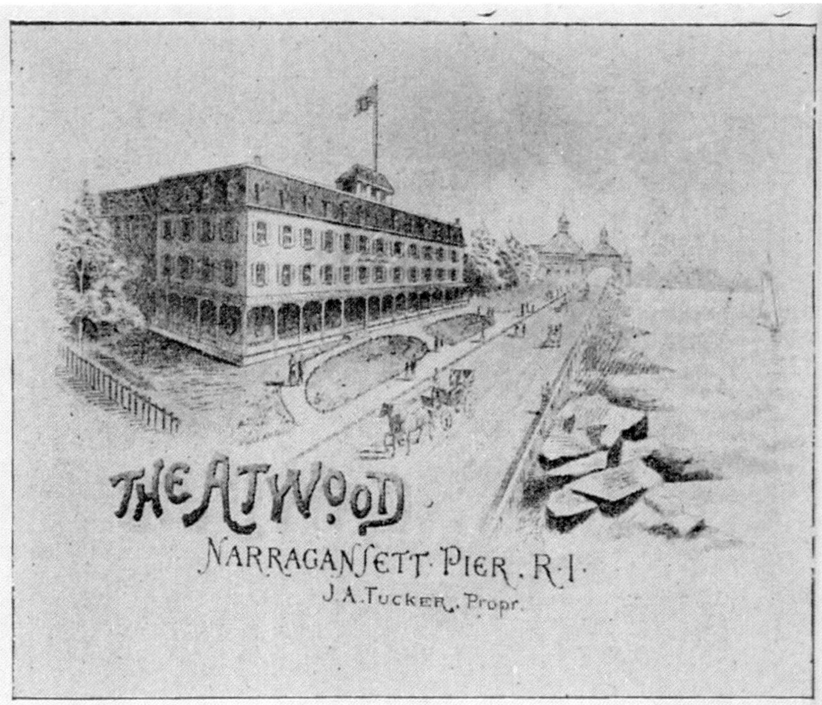

J. Alex. McClunie

LANDSCAPE ARCHITECT,

Furnishes Plans of Public Parks, Cemeteries, Private Grounds, etc.

Work Executed bv Contract or Otherwise.

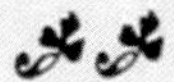

177 Asylum Street, Hartford, Conn.

NARRAGANSETT PIER.

☙ ☙ ☙

☙☙☙Near the western entrance to Narragansett Bay, about ten miles across the water from Newport, lies a city of hotels and cottages which, with Block Island, Watch Hill and Newport, has made Rhode Island the most famous of all American seacoast hotel resorts.☙☙☙It has accommodations for neariy 4,000 guests, a capacity more than double that of the hostelries at the " City by the Sea."☙It is the favorite summer home of Western and Southern people, and attracts largely from New York city and the Middle States,☙☙☙So deeply is it enshrined in the esteem of its older patrons that many have returned season after season, and finally erecting villas in desirable locations where they may from their own verandas enjoy the refreshing breezes and the grand ocean views.☙The greatest attraction at the Pier is the magnificent beach just north of the hotels.☙☙It is about a mile in length, crescent-shaped, smooth and hard.☙☙At mid-day, during the fashionable bathing hours, the scene presented is a lively and animated one.☙The costumes of the bathers are varied and picturesque.☙☙The next prominent features in the natural attractions are the bold rugged rocks along the coast.☙The drives about this vicinity are interesting and romantic.☙

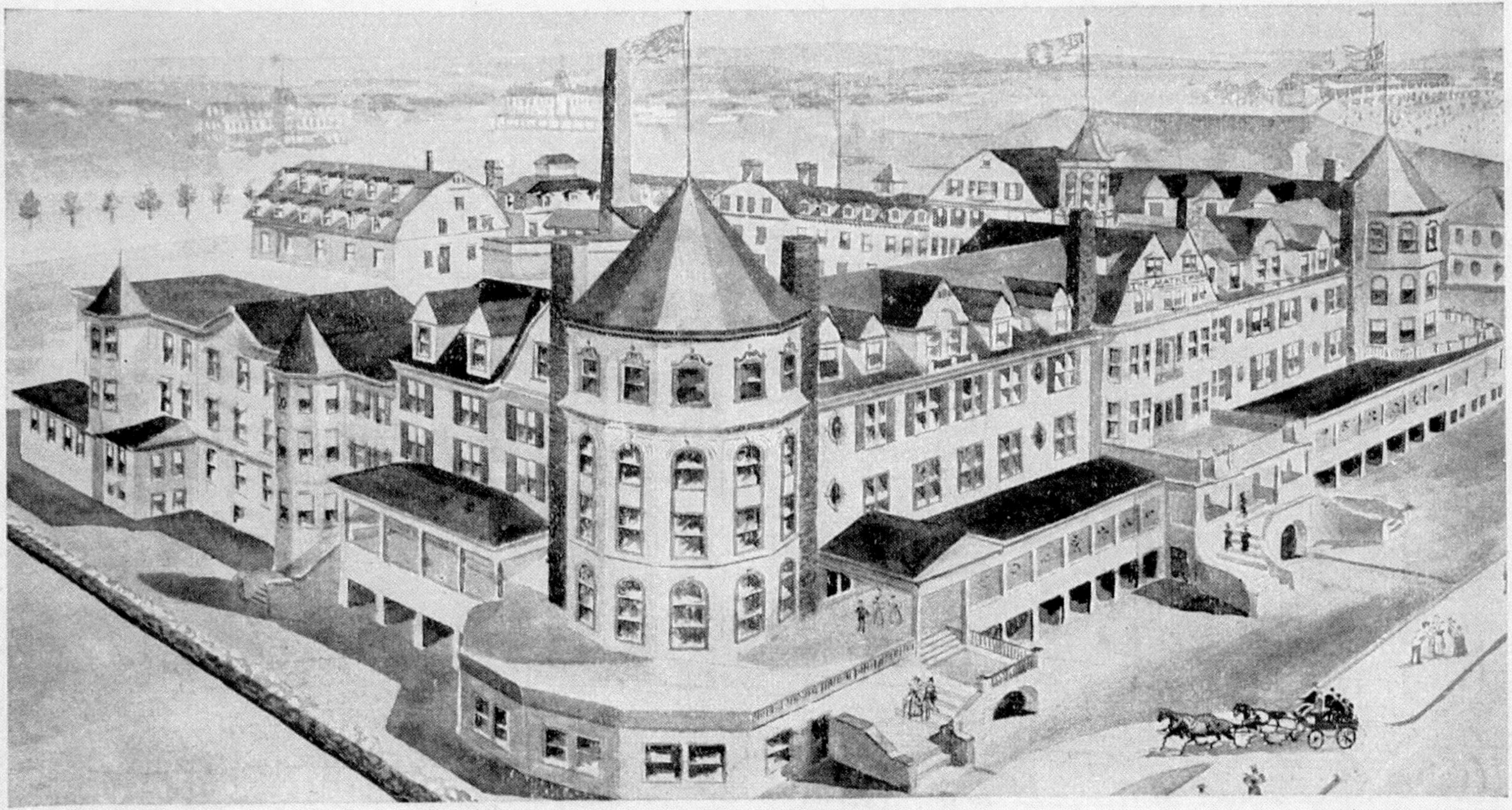

THE NEW MATHEWSON HOUSE, NARRAGANSETT PIER.

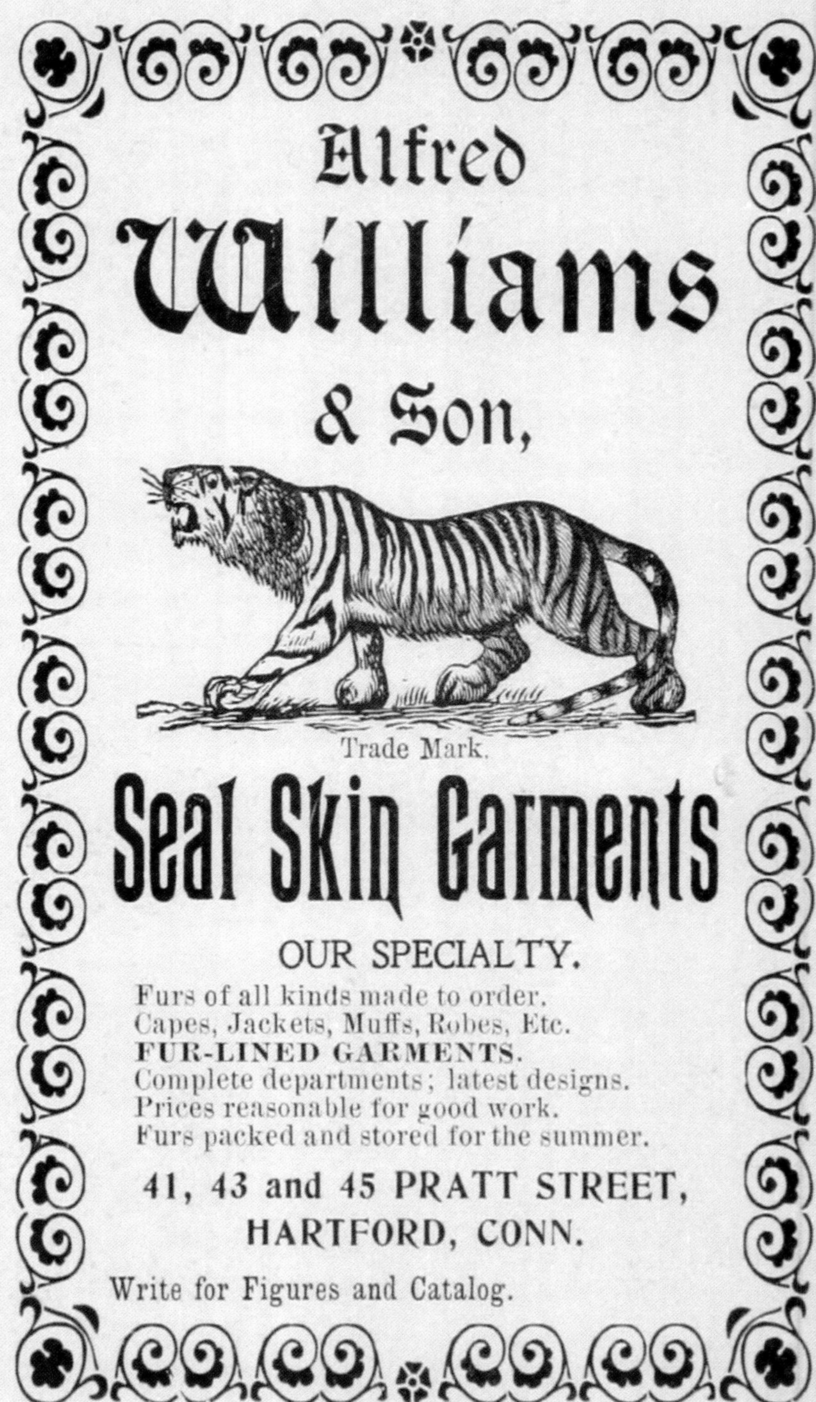
Alfred
Williams
& Son,
Trade Mark.
Seal Skin Garments
OUR SPECIALTY.
Furs of all kinds made to order.
Capes, Jackets, Muffs, Robes, Etc.
FUR-LINED GARMENTS.
Complete departments; latest designs.
Prices reasonable for good work.
Furs packed and stored for the summer.
41, 43 and 45 PRATT STREET,
HARTFORD, CONN.
Write for Figures and Catalog.

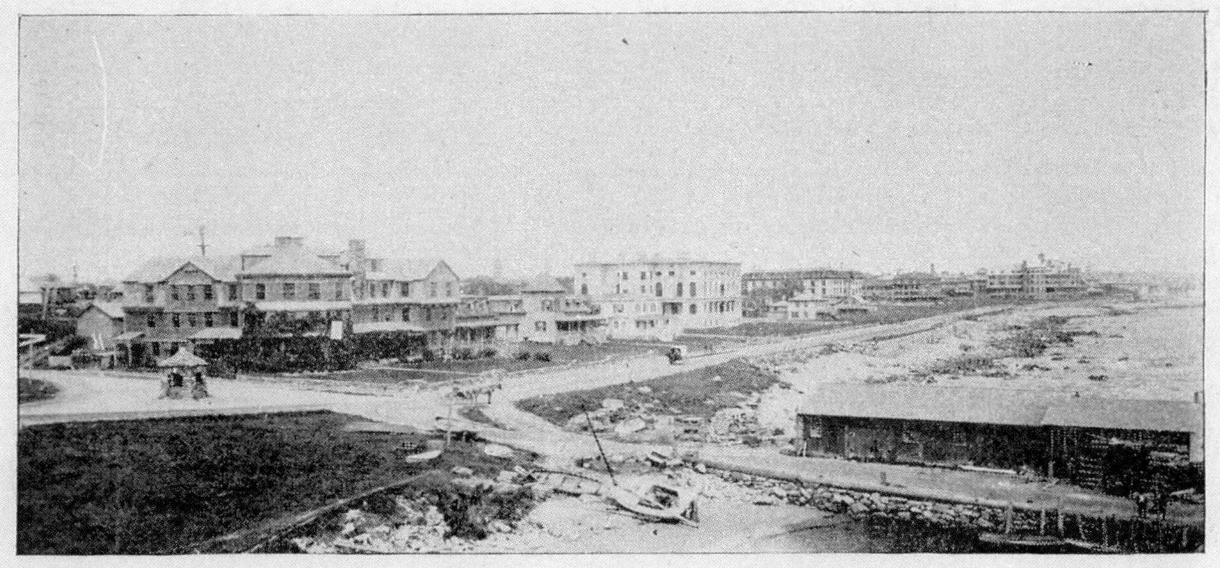

THE OCEAN FRONT,

Narragansett Pier.

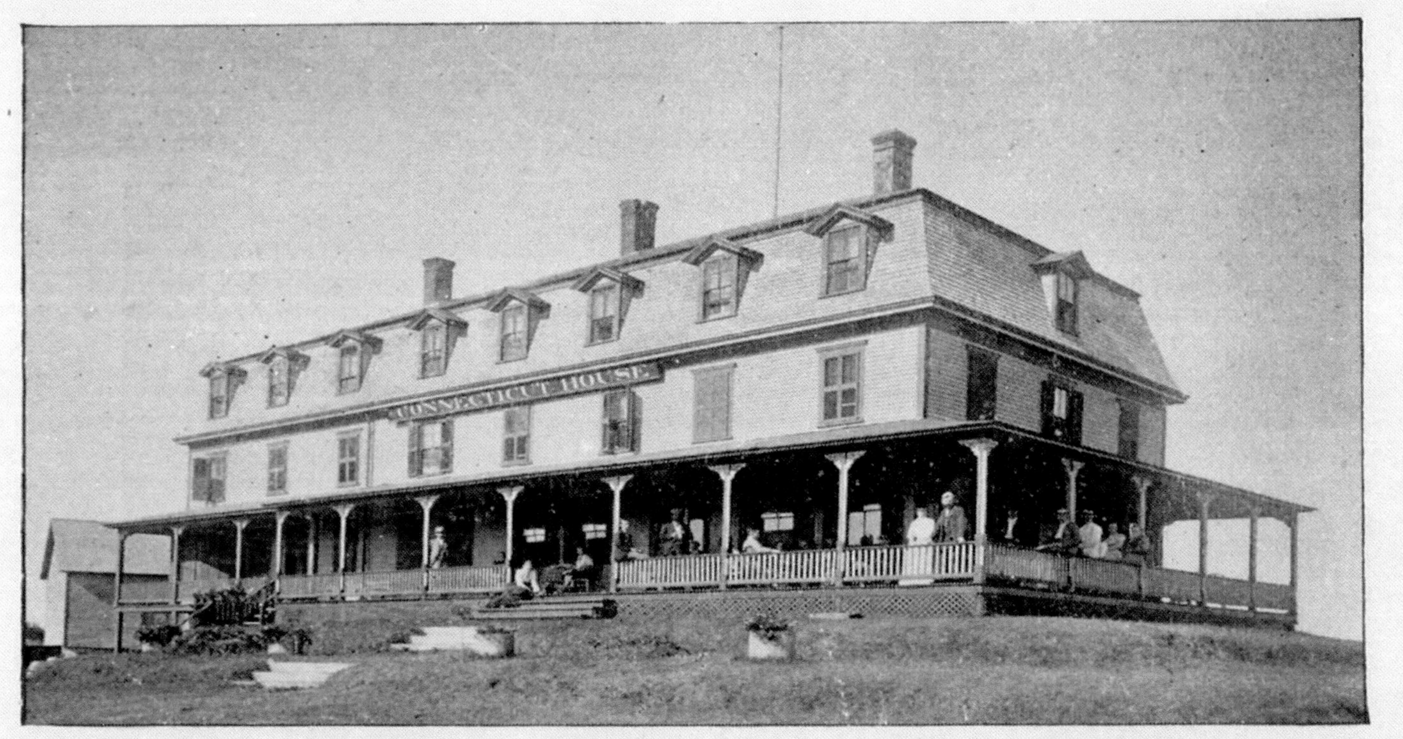

THE CONNECTICUT HOUSE, Block Island.

Charmingly situated on high ground, about midway between the old and new harbors, Large, airy, well furnished rooms; free carriage from all boats; near bathing beach; fine ocean view; carriages and boats at the service of guests. Terms reasonable. Address

E. H. DAY, Manager.

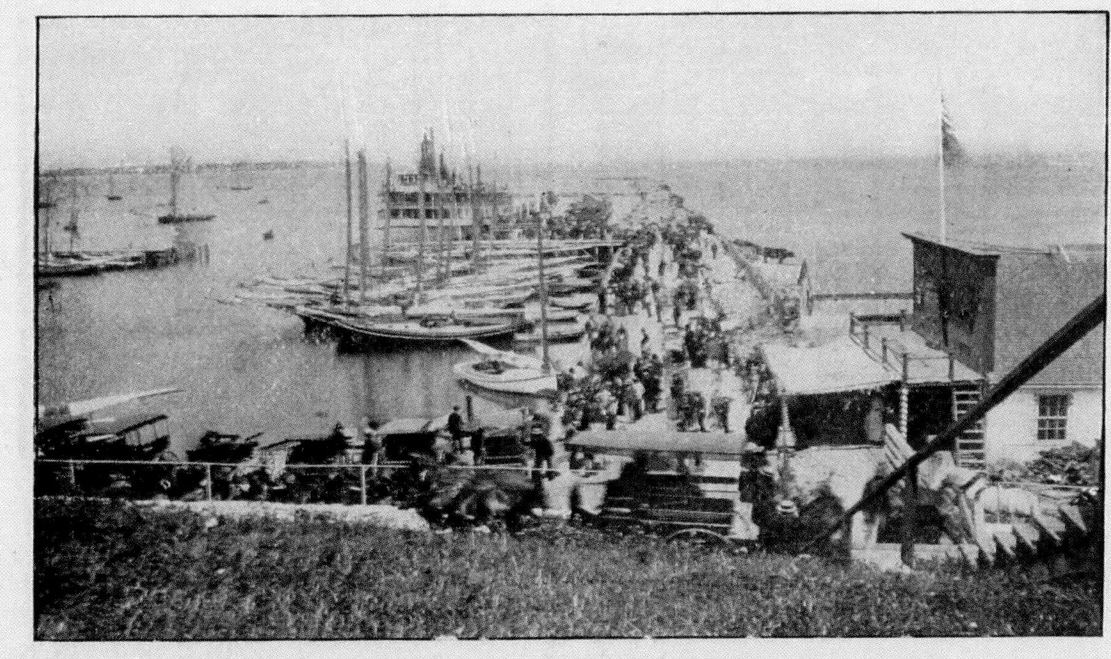

THE BREAKWATER, BLOCK ISLAND.

Select a nice Souvenir of your visit from the

Bric-a-Brac, Curios, 

Sea Specimens, Etc.

At the General Supply Store of

C. C. BALL,

Facing the Landing, and near Leading Hotels

Island Agent for the "Narragansett Blue Book."

BLOCK ISLAND.

Tinned Meats and Lunch Delicacies for YACHTING, FISHING and PIC-NIC PARTIES.

Choice Fruits, Toilet Articles, Stationery, Perfumery, Etc.
Yachts supplied with **Ice, Coal** and **Water.**

The Seaside House

Service most Homelike.

Block Island.

Prices Reasonable.

Midway between the Old and New Harbors.
Nearest the Bath Houses.

Address, CAPT. FRANCIS WILLIS, Proprietor.

Union House

On elevated land, near Steamboat Landing, Post-Office, Telegraph Offices, Etc.

Shaded Lawn; Location Unrivaled. Well Furnished Rooms, Liberal Table, Reasonable Rates.

Write to or call on **L. A. BALL, Proprietor, Block Island.**

BLOCK ISLAND.

☙ ☙ ☙

☙☙☙The little spot on the map of Rhode Island, midway between Point Judith and Montauk Point, conveys to the observer no conception of the beauties of the verdure-clad island which has become the summer home of thousands of delighted visitors.☙☙It is only after one has passed the surf-beaten shores that the beauties of this bit of nature's handiwork are fully revealed, and although the view from the steamer as it approaches the harbor in a measure prepares the visitor for what is to come, it is only on a closer acquaintance with the grassy slopes, the winding roads and the music of old ocean's surges that one understands why this bit of sea-washed earth has become so dear to those who year after year visit its shores.☙The harbor or basin, which is the landing place of the steamers from Narragansett Bay and Newport, is on the east side of the island at the southern extremity of a long crescent shaped strip of sandy beach, and is enclosed and protected by a breakwater of stone, constructed at great expense by the government, forming a refuge for coastwise vessels whose course brings them to the vicinity of the island.☙☙On the gentle slopes overlooking the breakwater and scattered for

Fifteen Miles at Sea. The Bermuda of the North.

Daily Steamers from New York, New London.

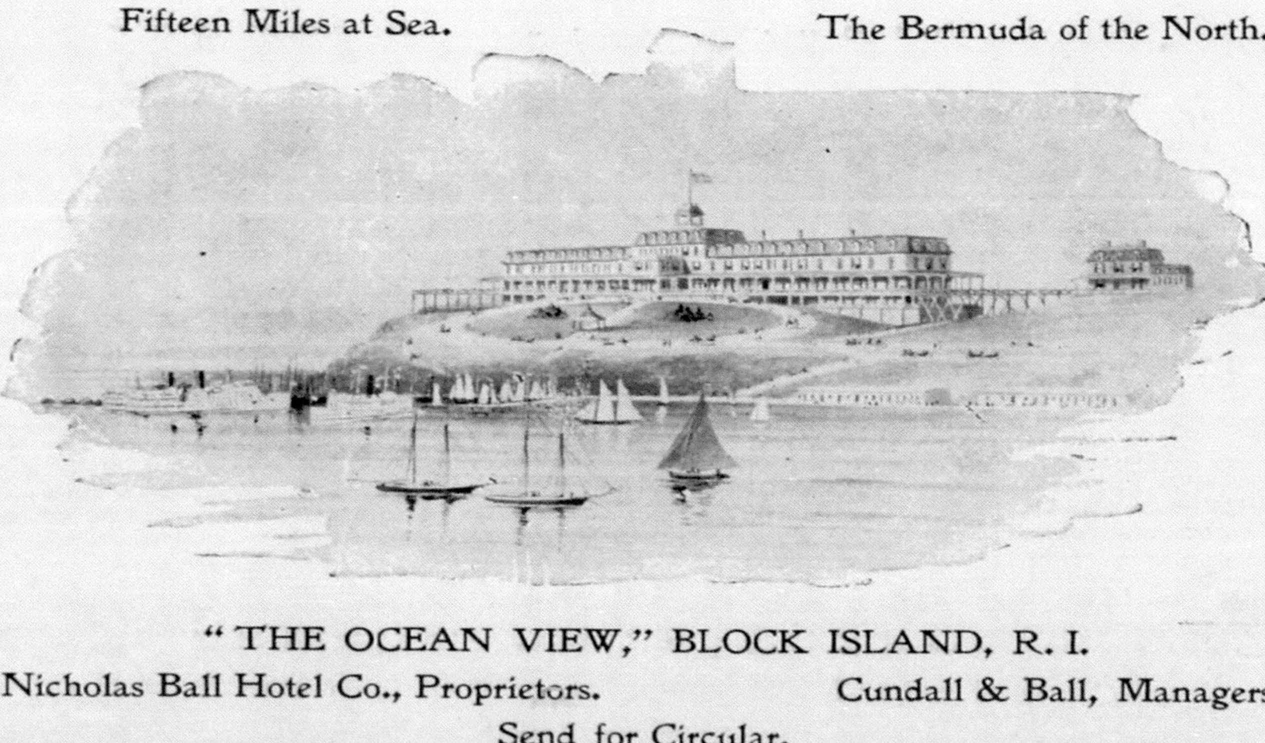

Daily Steamers from Providence, Newport.

"THE OCEAN VIEW," BLOCK ISLAND, R. I.

Nicholas Ball Hotel Co., Proprietors. Cundall & Ball, Managers.

Send for Circular.

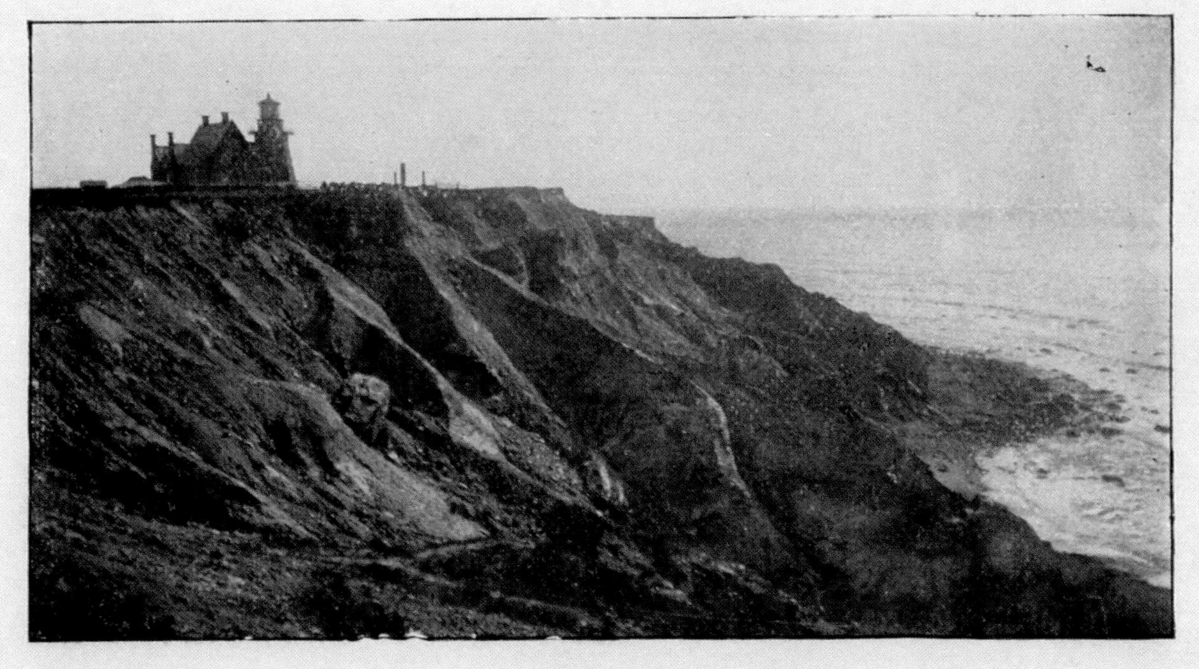

THE BLUFFS AND UNITED STATES LIGHTHOUSE,

Block Island.

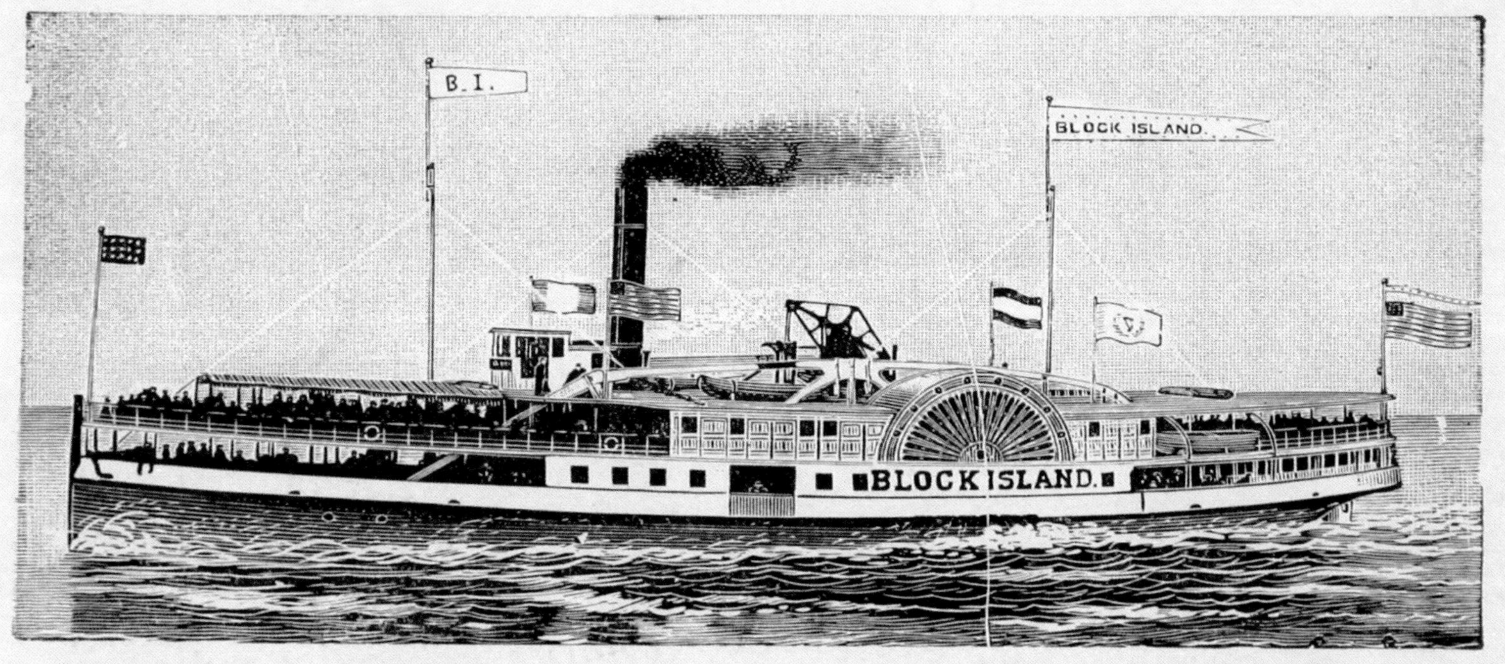

The most expeditious route to Block Island and Watch Hill is via the New London Steamboat Company's elegant steamer,

☘☘☘☘☘☘ "BLOCK ISLAND." ☘☘☘☘☘☘

SEASON OF 1896.—Commencing June 29th, this favorite steamer will leave New London daily (Sundays excepted) at 9.45 a. m.; Watch Hill, 10.55; arrive at New Harbor, Block Island, 12.30 p. m. Returning, leave New Harbor, Block Island, 2.30 p. m.; Watch Hill, 3.30; arriving at New London, 5.00. Connection made at New London with trains of Central Vermont and New York, New Haven & Hartford Railroads, and New York steamers of Norwich Line.

D. MACKENZIE, General Manager. J. A. SOUTHARD, General Passenger Agt.

❧ ❧ ❧

a mile or more on or near the eastern shore are upwards of twenty hotels and numerous cottages of varying capacity, most of the proprietors of which are residents, and whose tables are supplied with the freshest of vegetables from the adjacent farms and gardens and with fish caught in many cases in plain view from the piazzas.❧❧❧The surface of the island is undulating, the highest elevation, Beacon Hill, being 211 feet above the sea level.❧❧ On its summit is an observatory, from which in fine weather the main land and Montauk Point on the eastern end of Long Island may be seen, while the surface of the entire island with its grassy slopes and innumerable ponds is brought within the view of the observer.❧❧The largest of these lakelets is the Great Salt Pond, situated about a mile from the breakwater and just north of the centre of the island. ❧In this pond which contains over a thousand acres and nearly divides the island in two parts, a new harbor has been formed with a depth of from 12 to 60 feet and of sufficient size for a fleet to ride at anchor.❧Access to its waters is provided ba a channel 600 feet in width, with a depth of 16 feet, which has been cut through the narrow strip of sand which

separates it from the ocean on the northwest, and which is protected by a breakwater now in course of construction on either side. At the south of the new harbor, at the end of a pleasant road leading to the hotels and principal stores, a substantial pier has been constructed which is the landing place of the steamers from New London and from New York via Sag Harbor. The new harbor is perfectly sheltered in all weathers, and it is claimed that a saving of from 25 to 45 minutes results from its use by these lines. Among the island's attractions are the U. S. Lighthouse and great steam foghorn on the summit of the south cliffs, the cliffs themselves with a sheer descent of nearly 200 feet, and the splendid bathing beach with commodious bath-houses near all the principal hotels. In the waters sea bass, cod, mackerel and many other varieties of fish tempt the angler, while hops at the hotels, lawn tennis, etc., serve to prevent the possibility of ennui. With its great natural attractions and the increased facilities for reaching its shores, it is not strange that Block Island has become one of the most popular summer resorts on the Atlantic coast. Its hotel accommodations are of the very best.

Block Island Steamboat Company.

Popular Line between Providence and Block Island, via Newport and Providence, Fall River & Newport Steamboat Company. ☘☘ Carrying the United States Mail. ☘☘

THE STAUNCH STEAMER

"G. W. DANIELSON"

CAPTAIN CONLEY.

Daily, Sundays excepted, between Block Island and Newport, connecting with the Providence, Fall River and Newport Steamers, leaving Block Island at 7.15 A. M., and at Newport 1.30 P. M. All express matter for Block Island will be shipped by Earle & Prew's Express; all freight to be marked "Block Island, via. P., F. R. & N. Stbt. Co."

Winter Time-Table.—Leave Block Island Monday, Wednesday and Friday at 8.30 A. M. Returning, leave Providence Tuesday and Saturday at 9.00 A. M.; Newport, Tuesday, Thursday and Saturday, at 12.30 P. M.

Block Island House, Block Island.

This hotel overlooks all others on the Island. From it the views of the ocean are magnificent. The hotel is about half a mile, by a good road, from the landing, and a carriage is in waiting on the arrival of the boat.

CAPT. GEO. W. CONLEY, Proprietor.

(Of Steamer Danielson.)

NARRAGANSETT PIER RAILROAD.

From Narragansett Pier.

Sunday Trains on and after June 28.

Train Nos.	1		5	7	9	13	15	17	19	21	23	25	27	31	33	35	37	39
LEAVE	A M	A M	A M	A M	A M	P M	P M	P M	P M	P M	P M	P M	P M	A M	A M	P M	P M	P M
Narr. Pier..........	7 10	7 40	9 05	10 15	11 20	12 20	2 00	3 40	4 40	6 00	6 10	7 35	8 35	8 25	9 25	3 45	6 15	7 10
Wakefield..........	7 18	7 48	9 13	10 23	11 27	12 28	2 07	3 48	4 48	6 08	6 18	7 43	8 43	8 33	9 33	3 53	6 23	7 18
Peacedale..........	7 21	7 51	9 16	10 26	11 30	12 31	2 10	3 51	4 51	6 11	6 21	7 46	8 46	8 36	9 36	3 56	6 26	7 21
Kingston ...Arrive	7 36	8 05	9 30	10 41	11 45	...	2 23	4 05	5 00	...	6 36	8 01	...	8 51	...	4 08	6 41	...
Wickford Junction	8 06	8 23	9 49	11 22	12 56	...	2 49	5 03	5 42	...	7 49	...	...	9 08	...	4 44		...
Providence.........	8 50	8 55	10 40	11 57	1 50	...	3 24	5 55	6 15	...	7 24	...	...	9 50	...	5 35	...	...
Boston....	10 15	10 15	1 15	1 15	3 15	...	4 30	7 15	7 25	...	8 30	...	...	12 00	...	7 40	...	...
Worcester......	10 45	10 45	1 20	3 07	...	...	6 00		10 05	...	...	...	...	...	...	7 50	...	...
Wood River Jc. arr	8 02	8 56	...	11 16	...	...	2 45	...	5 32	...	...	8 21	...	9 16	...	4 28	...	10 26
Westerly..........	8 21	9 12	...	11 32	12 22	...	3 01	4 42	5 49	...	...	8 43	...	9 34	...	4 46	7 10	10 48
Stonington.........	8 30	9 21	...	11 40	12 31	...	3 12	4 51	6 05	...	...	8 55	...	9 42		4 55	...	11 03
New London...	9 00	9 50	...	11 40	12 58	...	3 40	5 20	6 40	...	...	P M	...	10 15	...	5 30	7 40	P M
New Haven	...	11 52	...	1 00	2 25	...	5 25	7 05	9 05	...	...	...	...	...	...	7 05	9 05	...
New York (Sh. Line)	...	2 00	...	3 30	4 30	...	7 30	9 00	11 00	...	...	...	...	...	...	9 00	11 00	...
New York (St. Line)	...	...	...	...	...	...	...	...	...	...	...	6 00	...	...	...	...	...	6 00

To Narragansett Pier.

Sunday Trains, on and after June 28.

Train Nos.	2	4	6	8	10	12	14	16	20	22	24	26	28	30	32	34	36	38
LEAVE	A M	A M	P M	P M	A M	A M	A M	P M	A M	P M	P M	P M	P M	A M	A M	P M	P M	P M
New York (St. Line)	...	...	6 00	6 00	...	...	...	...	...	...	...	...	...	...	...	...	...	...
New York (Sh. Line)	...	...	...	...	...	5 00	...	...	10 02	...	1 02	...	3 00	...	...	...	...	...
New Haven..........	...	...	A M	A M	...	7 50	...	...	12 05	...	3 00	4 20	4 55	...	...	...	...	...
New London.	...	...	6 30	7 00	...	10 05	...	...	1 34	...	4 27	5 45	6 25	...	7 30	...	3 05	...
Stonington........	...	...	7 02	7 33	...	10 30	...	...	2 08	...	4 52	6 09	6 54	...	8 06	...	3 39	...
Westerly	...	...	7 14	7 43	...	10 39	...	...	2 07	...	5 01	...	7 04	...	8 18	...	3 51	...
Wood River Junc..	...	...	7 33	...	...	10 54	...	...	2 36	...	4 29	...	7 19	...	8 36	...	4 09	...
Worcester	...	...	...	...	...	6 45	9 36	...	11 45	...	2 35	...	4 00	...	...	...	...	...
Boston	...	...	...	...	...	9 00	10 03	...	1 03	...	3 00	...	5 45	...	...	...	1 00	5 00
Providence........	...	...	6 40	...	7 30	10 10	11 19	...	2 09	3 30	4 15	...	7 05	...	8 00	...	3 20	6 04
Wickford Junc.	...	...	7 25	...	8 16	10 48	11 40	...	2 40	4 02	4 58	...	7 47	...	8 43	...	3 59	...
Kingston..........			7 53	8 10	9 35	11 09	11 55	...	2 54	4 15	5 29	6 42	8 06	...	9 00	...	4 30	6 45
Peacedale.........	6 30	7 21	8 15	8 22	9 47	11 20	12 07	1 40	3 06	4 25	5 41	6 54	8 18	8 05	9 12	3 20	4 42	6 57
Wakefield.........	6 33	7 24	8 18	8 25	9 50	11 33	12 10	1 43	3 09	4 28	5 44	6 57	8 21	8 08	9 15	3 23	4 45	7 00
Narragans't P. Arr.	6 41	7 32	8 25	8 33	9 58	11 41	12 18	1 51	3 16	4 35	5 52	7 05	8 29	8 16	9 23	3 31	4 53	7 08

Time Table commencing June 18, 1896.

G. T. LANPHEAR, SUPT.